MODERN FOOTBALL STILL IS RUBBISH

Slinging mud at what's left of 'the beautiful game'

MODERN FOOTBALL STILL IS RUBBISH

Slinging mud at what's left of 'the beautiful game'

Nick Davidson
& Shaun Hunt

SPORTS
BOOKS

Published in Great Britain by
SportsBooks Limited
PO Box 422
Cheltenham
GL50 2YN
Tel: 01242 256755
email: info@sportsbooks.ltd.uk
www.sportsbooks.ltd.uk

Cover design by Nick Davidson

A catalogue record for this book is available from the British Library.

ISBN 978 1899807 90 1

Printed in the UK by CPI Bookmarque, Croydon, CRO 4TD

Nick would like to thank all the children of the MFIR revolution. You know who you are. Gegen den modernen Fußball. Forza Sankt Pauli.

Shaun would like to thank all his family and friends who gave so much support throughout. YNWA. Special thanks to Derek Marsden (Phoenix from comicsuk) for help with The Cannonball Kid.

Nick and Shaun would both like to thank to our publisher, Randall Northam – without his vision the contents of this book (and the previous one) would be confined to a car park in Coventry where so much of it was conceived.

Against Modern Football

We knew we were onto *something* when we wrote the first book. Sure, we were labelled the 'grumpy old men of football', but it wasn't just the misplaced nostalgia and the inability to come to terms with life in the 21st century that drove us on – we knew we weren't alone. We knew there were thousands of people out there sick to the back teeth of the modern game. You only have to tune in to *606* or spend five minutes on a football messageboard to realise the extent of the malaise. The football we knew was eating itself – gorging on a feast of television money and self-importance.

That said, we weren't touting ourselves as suburban prophets – radical visionaries here to reclaim football for the working man (well, not out loud at least). We knew our words wouldn't change a thing. After all, football fans are a disparate bunch, divided by decades of local, regional and international rivalry – they couldn't possibly come together to fight the moneymen intent on ruining the modern game.

But then, while surfing the internet, we stumbled across a series of articles about the 'No al Calcio Moderno' movement. No al Calcio Moderno (rough translation, 'Against Modern Football') began at the end of the 1990s among the ultra groups of Italian football. Although championed most passionately by the Antifa Ultras – a broad coalition of left-wing fan groups who take a radical stance against racism, fascism and commercialism in football – the No al Calcio Moderno movement has transcended the traditional left/right ultra division and united fan groups across Italian football.

We hadn't been so excited by a political movement since our short-lived attempt to run for parliament as founder members of the Alliance of Rainbow Socialist Entities (think about it) in the early '90s. Here was a significant body of fans that shared our ideals.

No al Calcio Moderno banners have appeared at grounds all over Italy as fans react against: increased commercialisation; all-seater stadiums; rip-off ticket prices; ridiculous kick-off times that are dictated by the television companies; heavy-handed policing; and players bought and sold like merchandise. The movement has spread across Europe to the Bundesliga with *Gegen den Modernen Fussball* becoming a rallying cry for German football fans.

The ultra scene in Germany doesn't have the same reputation for lapsing into violence as its Italian counterpart – but it is equally political. Supporters across the country have protested fervently against modern football. Bayern Munich's ultras even compared themselves to the oppressed Tibetan people with a banner at the Alliance Arena reading, 'In Tibet and here: freedom instead of a police state'. When FC St Pauli took on 1860 Munich in the dreaded Monday night television slot, a spectacular protest against the broadcaster, DSF, took place. Banners proclaiming, 'Scheiss DSF' (you can work it out) littered the ground, and a chant of the same was clearly audible for the entire first half. The protest was so successful that, suitably embarrassed, DSF didn't show FC St Pauli at home on a Monday night for the rest of the 2007/08 season. Just imagine protests on a similar scale against Sky in this country? Richard Keys would be tearing his hair out.

Television is of great significance for Germany's fan groups. The 2009/10 season has seen large swathes of football coverage fall under Sky's remit and with it the very real prospect of Bundesliga matches spread out across the weekend in a similar fashion to the UK. But unlike the passive acceptance of British fans, supporters *Gegen den Modernen Fussball* have rallied behind the *Ohne Uns Kein Kick* (*Without Us No Game*) campaign. They want to see a return to the traditional 15.30 Saturday kick-offs and have launched regular protests at matches and a postcard campaign that could see 250,000 cards arriving on the doorstep of the German broadcaster. If successful in forcing DSF to compromise over fixtures it would be a landmark victory for football fans not just in Germany but across the globe.

Our European comrades have restored our faith and given us hope. They have reminded us that it is possible to facilitate change and claim the game back from the money-men. If fans in Germany and Italy can dispense with petty rivalries and unite for the good of the game then, surely, we can put down the remote control, get out of our armchairs and fight for the game we love?

Is being Against Modern Football just misplaced nostalgia? We don't think so.

Anthem jackets

When is a tracksuit top not a tracksuit top? When it's a sodding 'anthem jacket'.

We first noticed this phenomenon as the camera lingered on England's players lining up in the bowels of Wembley Stadium prior to the friendly against Slovakia in 2009. The game had been chosen to launch England's latest kit, and the design of the new shirt had been shrouded in secrecy. Obviously, the shirt had to be properly unveiled and the tunnel at Wembley was not an appropriate location. The big reveal had to happen out on the pitch. So, how to get the new shirt out there without anyone noticing? Easy, tracky tops.

But tracksuit tops are mundane, functional garments and not exactly aspirational. You can almost picture the panic and the frantic scratching of heads in the weekly marketing meetings as the day of the kit launch approached. At least until some bright spark piped-up: 'Anthems! They have to play the bloody national anthems!' Genius. 'We'll clothe them in chav-tastic white tracky-tops, but we'll call them "anthem jackets", and they sell by the bucket load down at JD Sports!'

Problem solved. That's what we thought, anyway. But then we discovered that anthem jackets have been around for ages. England's kit launch was just the first time they'd appeared on our radar. We are so hopelessly out of touch. That tatty, old zip-up top you've been wearing to football on a Sunday morning for the last 15 years? Think of it as an anthem jacket, and consider yourself an avant-garde fashionista.

Beautiful Goal!, The

When FIFA announced plans to award a trophy to the player who scores the most beautiful goal of the year, we got all excited. The FIFA Puskás Award is awarded in memory of the legendary Hungarian striker Ferenc Puskás.

At first we thought this was a wonderful initiative, but we've become increasingly concerned that not all goals will have an equal chance to qualify. We don't like to blow our own trumpet, but we have scored some cracking goals at five-a-side this year. Unfortunately, there were no cameras to record them. We are thinking of sending in a storyboard to Sepp Blatter, so that he can have a look at a few of them. One even secured us a place in the knockout stages of the Cup competition but nobody thought to record it, not even on a shaky mobile phone. We are sure we are not alone. There are millions of great goals scored every week, but only a select few are broadcast. It's okay, if you play in one of Europe's top leagues, but what if your goal is scored on pitch 17 at Hackney Marshes? Surely, if it's that good it should at least make the shortlist?

Of course, not so long ago, even professional games went unrecorded – unthinkable, now in the satellite age, but true. Back in 1985, Jan Molby scored what is considered to be one the best goals ever seen at Anfield in a League Cup game against Manchester United. There were no TV cameras present, but Jan claims to have a copy on video, filmed by a police surveillance camera and given to him by Ron Atkinson. This raises many questions? Why did Ron Atkinson have a videotape of the police surveillance camera in the first place? And why was the camera pointed at the pitch? Who knows? But it does makes us wonder whether Sepp would find CCTV footage as beautiful?

The winner of The Beautiful Goal will probably come from an international or European game, given the significance and exposure these matches are afforded. But what about us? We are prepared to courier our goal storyboards to FIFA HQ at our own expense. We would even consider a personal representation to Sepp, perhaps involving us re-enacting our beautiful goal through expressive dance. We just want to be given the chance. Just because a goal isn't captured on TV, doesn't mean it's not beautiful. And anyway, five overweight blokes in leotards prancing about like lunatics should more than make up for a lack of actual footage.

Binders/The Collection

It's not like the world is short of rubbish hooligan movies. So we were downright astonished when we heard they were remaking the 1989, made for TV, knuckle dust-up, *The Firm*. How could they possibly improve on perfection? And would Gary Oldman get to reprise his role as hoolie-in-chief, Bex Bissell?

From *The Football Factory* to *Cass* via *Green Street* this curious film sub-genre ('casual-slasher' movies, anyone?) havs certain things in common: the glorification of violence, minimal plot and, in most cases, Danny Dyer.*

The new version of *The Firm* took a bit of a critical mauling, but to us it just seemed to be a 90-minute advert for sportswear giants, Fila and Sergio Tacchini. Of course, *The Firm* is more than just casual product placement. The official synopsis of the film describes it as: 'Humorous, heart warming and set to a killer jazz funk '80s soundtrack.' That's a soundtrack including both Jermaine Jackson's *Let's Get Serious* and Nik Kershaw's *The Riddle*. 'Nuff said.

But we are not here for a *The Late Show*-esque critical appraisal of hooligan flicks – we're here to nab our own movie deal. We can't help thinking that the film industry has missed a trick. So forgive us, while we fine-tune a pitch for our culturally significant coming-of-age movie.

Over the years, the British film industry has picked apart and reassembled almost every aspect of youth culture. Aside from the rom-com shenanigans of *Notting Hill* and *Four Weddings and a Funeral*, these gritty, rites-of-passage movies are what we do best. There's a long lineage that spans the decades and includes the likes of *Cathy Come Home*, *Trainspotting* and *This is England* – films that document the trials of working-class youth.

On the subject of *Trainspotting*, Nick was probably the only person in the country hugely disappointed that it was a movie about drugs and not an edge-of-the-platform thriller about the devastating consequences of The Beeching Report.

So, it is time the real story of football's underground was told. And we are the perfect people to document this cultural phenomenon because – *we* lived it. We guarantee for every one casual hooligan there were ten of *our* number. We too had our own music and clothes (although calling it 'fashion' might be stretching it a bit.) *We* were *The Programme Collectors*.

Yep, that's right – we collected football programmes. And we kept them in plastic wallets inside numbered binders. Often we acted alone, but occasionally we would come together in a distinctly tribal gathering – usually held in a musty town hall somewhere in the East Midlands. We'd convene for a programme fair.

We too had our generals and our top boys. The generals were usually men of advancing years and had no traceable next of kin; men who worked in the dusty recess of local government by day, but at night returned to their maisonettes in the suburbs to leaf through their perfectly indexed back-catalogues of football programmes. At fairs, these generals could be found peddling their addictive, intoxicating fayre to the next generation of collectors – people like us, impressionable teenagers with few social skills, chronic acne and a snowball's chance in hell of getting a girlfriend.

At school we were picked on and laughed at, but in a hall full of trestle tables and men with personal hygiene issues we were the dog's bollocks. Dressed in the latest Avanti clobber from C&A, with a pair of iconic Golas on our feet and a crisp fiver in our pockets (to be spent wisely, and only after we'd done at least three, thorough circuits of all the exhibitors in the hall) we were invincible.

We can't decide whether to call our film *The Collectors* in a nod to *The Firm*, or try to get Kevin Sampson involved and call it something snappy like *Binders*. Either way, the only Stanley knife action will be the accidental slashing of a programme cover during the attempted removal and repair of a rusty staple.

We are still working on the plot, but we've got an inkling that it will centre around the search for an obscure South East Counties League programme, from 1981, featuring Spurs and Charlton. We have nailed the opening shot though: it's early morning; a lone figure emerges from the carriage of a British Rail train, heads out of the station and through a dismal post-industrial landscape. As he comes over the brow of the hill, dressed in light-grey ski-jacket and pleated trousers, he stops for a moment and asks a local youth for directions to the Hinckley Programme Fair. 'Fook off, loser!' comes the response. Our hero shrugs his shoulders and continues walking down the hill, safe in the knowledge that he'll soon be amongst his own number, and full of hope that today might be the day he gets his hands on that ellusive programme.

* Of course, the directors of hoolie-films are always quick to point out that they are not glorifying violence and that, actually, their work – despite the gory punch-ups – has a strong anti-violence message.

Bloodsport for all

Was there ever a more heart-warming sight in football than watching some old, gnarled centre-half contesting a header sporting a makeshift head bandage and a blood-soaked shirt? It wasn't pretty but it evoked something vaguely gladi-atorial in all of us – it made us believe that our players cared enough to put their bodies on the line for a point away at West Brom.

When it came to international football, bleeding pro-fusely was one of the few things we were actually any good at. Playing on with a ridiculous head injury was part of our national identity, a visual reminder that Johnny Foreigner may well be technically superior and more fun to watch, but he wouldn't actually bleed for his country. Think Mr Caged-Tiger himself, Terry Butcher, in that World Cup quali-fier against Sweden in 1989 – the thousand-yard stare, the bloodied shirt – he looked like he'd staggered off the set of *Hamburger Hill.* England needed a draw against Sweden to qualify for Italia '90, and a bit of blood wasn't going to stop Butcher from doing his duty.

Yes, those were the days – days when soldiering on with an open wound was a sign of bravery rather than stupidity; days that made you long for a clash of heads in the play-ground so that you could look vaguely heroic when you re-turned to class after break, dripping with blood.

It wasn't just Terry Butcher. There's that classic photo-graph of Paul Ince, crêpe bandage wrapped around his bonce, blood down his once white England shirt, as England ground out a 0-0 draw in Rome to qualify for France '98. England made it to the World Cup and the press had a field day, twittering on about 'Blood and Guts' and 'England's Lionheart,' while conveniently forgetting we were actually a bit crap.

These days, blood (and probably thunder) has been

banned from football at any level. It doesn't matter if you are an international hard-man or a primary school kid – the first whiff of blood and you are instructed to leave the field. The risks are just too great – hell, you could have sustained a particularly nasty *nosebleed*.

The official line is the risk of cross-infection. Physios have to don rubber gloves before they can reach for a can of deep heat. A bit of blood and they're probably supposed to wear one of those bio-suits the CIA used when they quarantined ET. It's pathetic; blood and guts used to be part of our matchday experience; now it has been sanitised by the health and safety mob.

Football needs to be careful. Boxing, which has undergone a similar sanitisation process in recent years, is losing fans hand-over-fist to the more brutal *Ultimate Fighting Championship* – a mixed martial arts contest, where pretty much anything goes. Perhaps football should follow suit? Put six footballers in a cage (with a ball) and only let them out when their shirts are soaked in blood – now, that would make fantastic telly.

Bottle Top Old Bill

There's a kids' programme on Channel Five called *Bottle Top Old Bill*. It's on at about six o'clock in the morning but despite the early start it always raises a laugh (we both have young children so we *have* to be up that early).

You see, we can't watch it without thinking of the army of health and safety jobsworths whose sole purpose in life is to stop you entering the ground with the lid to your plastic Coke bottle. Just imagine trying to enter a football stadium with a soft drink, some of which you might want to save for later?

Confiscating the bottle top isn't enough. Repeat offenders should face a 10-year stretch in a maximum-security prison. Not only that, but this rigorous enforcement leads to the dangerous practice of bottle top secretion.* Forget being a drugs mule and swallowing a kilo of heroin, that's got nothing on trying to 'pass' a bottle top in time for kick-off.

* Obviously, we would never condone such a practice, no matter how bad your addiction to fizzy pop.

Brand identity

Let's be upfront about this – we identify with Russell Brand. It must be something about his barnet (have you seen *our* hair?); formidable intellect; meandering wit and success with women. Stand the three of us in a room together and you struggle to tell us apart.

With so much in common, it's not surprising that Brand is one of the few celebrity football columnists we actually like. For starters he passes the JCL (Johnny Come Lately test): our Russ was a Chicken Run regular at Upton Park in his yoof. Second, in his *Guardian* column, he managed the sort of literary freebasing that we can only dream of. There's not many football columnists who effortlessly mixed Voltaire, Ginsberg and Lee Cattermole into the same paragraph – except, maybe, Harry Harris.

Russell Brand was rightly pilloried for his (not inconsiderable) role in the Andrew Sachs answerphone debacle, but we see through the tabloid hysteria: we see a lineage from Brand back to the pioneers of 1960s counter-culture; to the brilliant leftfield minds that created magazines like *Oz* and *IT*. We also see someone who knows his football – and someone who, despite the money, fame and adulation heaped upon him, openly admits to being in awe of Tony Cottee.

So in an age where any celebrity halfwit who's caught ten minutes of Chelsea v Manchester United on Sky has a newspaper column, Russell Brand stood extravagantly coiffured head and shoulders above the competition. Well, at least until he jacked it in…

However, there must be something in the water in East London, as another 'appy 'ammer and comic legend, Phill Jupitus has grasped the nettle. With Ol' Rusty tied up in Holywood (we'd imagine) Big Phill is the only celebrity scribe we can tolerate. Like Brand, Jupitus also knows his football onions and his weekly column in *The Times* often raises a laugh on a Monday morning. It leaves us wondering if the Upton Park faithful have thought about starting the chant: 'Stand-up, if you love our stand-ups?' Probably not.

Britain's Got Talent

Who really cares about the Olympics? The 100m can be quite fun, but it's over in a matter of seconds. Apart from that: blokes in helmets pedalling around a track? Adolescent diving sensations? Three-day eventing? Do us a ruddy favour.

The Olympics is the World Cup no one cares about, but it's coming to London, so we've all got to whip ourselves into a frenzy of faux-excitement. There's a village, a train line, a stadium and there's even *football*. And this is where the problems start. Ever since London successfully bid for the 2012 games the media in general, and radio phone-in programmes in particular, have been having a field day with the idea of Great Britain entering a football team.

Just in case you've not turned on your radio during the last five years, fielding a GB football team is not as simple as it seems. You see, in proper football, England, Scotland, Wales and Northen Ireland field separate teams – and there is real concern that fielding a combined British team could bring about the end of civilisation as we know it, or at the very least threaten the independence and integrity of the individual national FAs. Anyhow, with each individual Football Association nervously fingering a letter signed by Sepp Blatter, it looks like Team GB may just take to the field come 2012.

Trouble is, they are missing the point: even if we enter a team; even if Alex Ferguson is manager; even if David Beckham is made captain; even if, by some miracle, Team GB wins the bloody tournament – no one will give a monkey's. Why not? 'Cos it's Olympic football. Only Brazil and Argentina take the competition vaguely seriously. For the rest of the world, it's the global equivalent of the Zenith Data Systems trophy. Do you think the Great British public will give a toss by the time the Olympics move on to Rio de Janeiro in 2016?

No. It's just a shallow attempt to garner more publicity for the London games.

Football is not an Olympic sport. Full stop. Then again, if we have to endure two more years of the Great British football debate, why don't we do things properly? Here's the plan:

Let's forget about footballers and instead fill the team with participants from *Britain's Got Talent*. We can see it now: Great Britain v South Korea kicks off with our entire team comprised of one of those young offenders' street dance ensembles that Simon Cowell is so fond of. Instead of defending, they transform themselves into a giant moving wave, drawing gasps of delight from the watching crowd. Then, as the game continues we bring on a really bad ventriloquist and that woman who can sing a bit. Obviously, all matches would have to take place in the lucrative Saturday tea-time slot, but we're sure that could be arranged. And, of course, we'd get hammered, but think of the TV ratings. Cowell and Piers Morgan (see Pierless) could form a management duo to rival that of Steve Gritt and Alan Curbishley back in the day at Charlton. And Amanda Holden could be team physio. All we need to do now is find a role for Ant and Dec and we've finally sorted the Olympic football conundrum.

Camera Obscura

Outstanding goals come in all shapes and sizes – from Carlos Alberto's goal in the 1970 World Cup final against Italy (the culmination of amazing Brazilian teamwork) to Van Basten's impossible volley in the 1988 European Championships, via the individual brilliance of Maradona against England in '86 or George Weah for AC Milan against Verona.

But true greatness requires something more, something that makes the goal stick in the memory for ever. Flair, audacity, brilliance or controversy just aren't enough. To go down in history something out-of-the-ordinary has to happen.

We've already documented Trevor Brooking's 'stanchion-shot' in the World Cup qualifier against Hungary in Budapest in 1981, when Sir Trev managed not only to score a vital goal but also wedge the ball in the stanchion (see *Modern Football is Rubbish*). Now it is time to salute the only other goal we can think of that matches our criteria…

Ladies and gentlemen, we give you Ian Rush's second goal in the 1986 FA Cup final against Everton. What makes this goal so great? Sure, it sealed a 3-1 cup final victory over their Merseyside rivals and thus a league and cup double. But that's not the reason. No, Ian Rush achieves immortality for managing to knock over the camera that was sitting in the bottom corner of the Wembley goal.

'That' goal that has plagued Rush ever since. Even now, journalists are never interested in what it felt like to score a winning goal at Wembley or to secure the double in such dramatic circumstances. All they really want to know is, 'Were you aiming for the camera?' Whether by accident or design, Ian Rush's ability to smash an expensive-looking camera from 18 yards has put him up there on a pedestal with Sir Trevor Brooking – the only two men in the history of the game who can lay claim to scoring *truly* great goals.

Cannes you kick it?

Football and cinema have always been awkward bedfellows. We've written at length about the cinematic beauty of *Escape to Victory* (see *Modern Football is Rubbish*), but leaving John Huston's career-defining masterpiece aside (apparently, his next film was *Annie* – what a comedown!) there wasn't a lot else out there. *The Arsenal Stadium Mystery* was way before our time, which just left us with Brian Glover's infamous scene in *Kes*.

So, we'd never have thought that football would feature prominently at the Cannes Film Festival three times in the last four years. And not even in our wildest dreams did we imagine that Ken Loach would direct a film that had football at its very core. But both these things have happened.

As Loach was picking up the prestigious Palme d'Or at Cannes in 2006 for *The Wind That Shakes the Barley*, *Zidane, A 21st Century Portrait* was getting a festival airing, something Ken must have subconsciously clocked. The Zidane flick directed by Douglas Gordon and Philippe Parreno featured 17 synchronised cameras trained on Zizou during a game against Villareal at the Bernabéu in 2005. A curious film: the cameras follow Zidane and no one else for the duration of the game, or at least until he's sent off near the end. Minimal dialogue and music by Mogwai give the film a strangely hypnotic quality and almost make you forget you are watching a game of football. Our only criticism is the choice of match. Sure, Zizou scored and got sent off, but if only the game in question had been the 2006 World Cup final against Italy. Imagine watching both Zidane's outrageous fifth-minute penalty (chipped in off the crossbar) and *that* headbutt from 17 different camera angles and without the twitterings of John Motson and Mark Lawrenson? That would be simply divine.

Hot on the heels of *Zidane, A 21st Century Portrait* was

Maradona, a documentary made by Serbian filmmaker Emir Kusturica. The film debuted at Cannes in 2008, although reviews were somewhat mixed. Some felt that Kusturica was too in awe of Maradona to be objective, but objectivity wasn't really the point. The film set about perpetuating the legend of Maradona, building on his Messiah status with football fans the world over.

True, most English folk, particularly those of a patriotic bent who have still not recovered from 'The Hand of God', won't be so keen, but if you are intrigued by Maradona's recent anti-imperialist rhetoric and his friendship with Fidel Castro then this film is for you. A particularly amusing segment has a cartoon Diego ghosting past Maggie Thatcher, Prince Charles, the Queen, Tony Blair, Ronald Reagan and George W. Bush to the sound of the Sex Pistols' *God Save the Queen*. Maradona's battle with drugs and his weight are never fully addressed, and this leaves you feeling like you've watched the entire film wearing those special glasses they've started giving out at the cinema again – only in this instance they give the film a rose-tinted hue rather than a third dimension.

Before we return to the French Riviera for one final time, there is another football film that deserves recognition. It may not have debuted at Cannes, but *The Damned United* is another fine addition to the world of football cinema. Adapted from the acclaimed novel by David Peace, *The Damned United* dramatises Brian Clough's disastrous 44-day spell in charge of Leeds United. The book was heavily criticised by Clough's family, who said it bore little resemblance to the truth, and though the film took a slightly warmer tone, it largely stuck to Peace's version of events. Historical accuracy aside, as a piece of period drama, the film successfully recreates the look and feel of football in the 1970s. Chesterfield's Saltergate stadium was used to recreate the Baseball Ground, Bloomfield Road, Carrow Road and Wembley, while Michael Sheen, whose previous roles included

Kenneth Williams, Tony Blair, Nero and David Frost, played a faultless Brian Clough. Only Stephen Graham's Billy Bremner struggled to maintain the illusion of 1970s authenticity. One thing is for certain: *The Damned United* succeeded where countless others had failed – it successfully brought football back to the big screen.

Which brings us back to Cannes, and to Ken Loach. We could hardly contain our excitement when we heard Loach was making a film about football; when we heard it starred Eric Cantona we nearly wet ourselves. We've been long-time admirers of Ken Loach's socio-realist brand of cinema, something that started with the aforementioned *Kes*, and continued through much admired films like *Land and Freedom*, *Carla's Song* and *My Name is Joe*. Here was a filmmaker whose work had helped shape our beliefs and whose politics shone through in virtually everything he did – we couldn't wait to see his take on the beautiful game.

We weren't disappointed. It turns out that *Looking For Eric* wasn't actually Ken's idea; it was Cantona's. Eric had approached Loach with several ideas for films, one in particular centring on the relationship between Cantona and a fan. Though Ken wasn't sure this idea would work, he liked the concepts it embraced – the important role football plays in peoples' lives and the perception of modern footballers as celebrities. Working with writer Paul Laverty, *Looking For Eric* was born. It is a film about football; a film about obsession; it is also a film about friendship. Eric Bishop is a postman whose life is in turmoil. He can't sustain a relationship with anyone from his (second) wife to his teenage stepsons. He finds a degree of salvation through a combination of his mates and their humorous self-help group, smoking dope and Eric Cantona.

Eric Cantona comes to him initially as a cannabis-assisted vision. Cantona, playing himself, helps our struggling postie make sense of his disaster-strewn life by dispensing seagulls and trawler-era pearls of wisdom.

The film is as close to feelgood as (we suspect) Loach will ever get. The touch is light – as deft as a Cantona flick – and there's not a kung-fu kick in sight. We were eager to discover Loach's take on modern football, and it seems he has neatly sidestepped a lot of the issues that weigh us down. Instead of dwelling on the negative, Loach concentrates on the idea that football is – despite everything – still about the relationship between players and fans.

He celebrates the way football brings people from all walks of life together, how the game can still be a force for good. Loach himself comments: 'It's a film against individualism: we're stronger as a gang than we are on our own. You can be pretentious about this but it is about the solidarity of friends, which is epitomised in a crowd of football supporters.'

It's a point of view that has certainly made us think. We spend so much time ruminating on football's decline – set against a backdrop of a mythical golden age – that we forget what a force for good it can be. Whether it's meeting your mates down the pub, playing in the same five-a-side team or taking your old man to the match, football is, despite everything, a unifying force. You could argue that Ken is getting sentimental in his old age, but we don't think so. Loach has, through cinema, reminded us of something Shankly nailed decades before: football as a representation of socialism.

The words of Bill Shankly could equally be the words of Ken Loach: 'The socialism I believe in is everyone working for each other, everyone having a share of the rewards. It's the way I see football, the way I see life.' *Looking For Eric* is that sort of film: on one level a film about a depressed post-office worker mildly obsessed with Eric Cantona; on another level it's about community values and the solidarity of friendship.

Either way, it is great to see football back in the multiplex. It seems an awful long time since 1981, when we queued round the block at the Odeon to see Michael Caine, Pelé and Sylvester Stallone strut their stuff in *Escape to Victory* – but both *The Damned United* and *Looking For Eric* have made that wait worthwhile.

Can't see the wood for the trees

Raised on stories (and shaky Betamax video footage) of Pelé & Co. at Mexico 70 and fresh from the exploits of Zico, Falcao and Socrates at the 1982 World Cup in Spain (not the free-flowing football, you understand, but the ability to squeeze into those impossibly skimpy shorts), we found ourselves sat in a geography lesson, sometime in 1984, pondering the eternal question: why are Brazil so bloody good at football?

There just had to be an explanation. Then, without warning, it dropped into our laps: our slightly ditzy geography teacher (and yes, of course, we fancied her) hit us with an amazing revelation:

'The Brazilian rainforest is being destroyed at a rate of 14 football pitches a day.'

We let the sentence reverberate around our heads for a while, but it sort of made sense: 14 football pitches were being built in the Amazon rainforest every day. Heaven! Just imagine hacking through the jungle, stumbling into a clearing only to find a game of football taking place between bare-footed Brazilians – all showing off a variety of tricks and flicks.

But why use the word destroy, Miss? Surely, football pitches were the very lifeblood of Brazilian culture. We'd not got as far as the Brazilian economy or the complexities of international trade, we just thought they made a tidy sum by being bloody good at football. Still, it got us thinking: if we had that many football pitches in England, we too could be the best in the world.

We soon realised that things weren't that simple, but not before the thought of naked Amazonian beauties playing football on a sculpted football pitch on a plateau in the rainforest had got us through many dull lessons on plate tectonics. Crikey, even the Liberal Democrats would sweep to power if they included creating 14 football pitches a day in their manifesto. Nick Clegg in a yellow Brazil top on polling day, surrounded by a bevy of ladies wearing shirts tied in a raunchy knot exposing an eyeful of midriff – that would knock the stuffing out of anything Tory Central Office could muster. However, a word of caution before we get carried away: it has taken donkeys' years for the FA to decide to build a few new pitches at Burton, so the idea of '14-a-day' might cause a few raised eyebrows in Soho Square.

It is interesting that football pitches were decreed the official unit of measurement for rainforest destruction. We doubt many people could give you the minimum and maximum lengths of a football pitch, but as a visual reference it's dead easy to understand.* Please note, cricket and rugby fans, your sport wasn't chosen. We feel that the football pitch should replace the acre as the main unit of area. If a farmer tells you he has 18 acres, do you honestly have any idea what he means? Imagine how impressed you would be if the farmer told you he had 15 football pitches of land.

Having understood how important the Amazon rainforest is to the planet and being astounded at how fast it was being devastated, we have waited more than 20 years to hear one of John Craven's prettier replacements on *Newsround* tell us that it has finally disappeared. Imagine our consternation as we witness a string of celebrities on TV finding another *almost* extinct animal in the jungle. What? 14 pitches a day for 25 years and there's *still* some jungle left? We cannot stand one more David Attenborough wildlife series, or yet another pompous celebrity canoeing up the Amazon with only a 30-strong entourage of camera crew, stylists and agents for company. Only recently they found another 'lost' tribe. They are not lost, they bloody live there. Quite happily. We know something that would make them even happier though: one of those football pitches they were promised 25 years ago.

Well, look at that? We got through a whole article about rainforests and we didn't mention Sting or Tantric sex. Oh, darn it...

*The length of a full-size soccer pitch must be between 100 yards (90 metres) and 130 yards (120 metres) and the width between 50 yards (45 metres) and 100 yards (90 metres). It is not allowed to be square. So now you know.

Cars in the ground

Can you imagine a row of Renault Méganes parked at a jaunty angle behind the goal at The Emirates? It would never happen. But it did.

Cars in football grounds were a genuine 1970s curio. From Stamford Bridge to Wembley Stadium via The Shay in Halifax, cars in stadiums were commonplace – though, as kids, we never really understood why.

When we saw them on the telly at Wembley we assumed they were leftovers from the stadium's ill-advised dalliance with stock-car racing (in the summer of 1974 two stock car meetings were held at Wembley with drivers lured by the £500 prize money and fans by the possible appearance of Radio One breakfast DJ, Noel Edmonds).

When we saw a single vehicle parked at other grounds, we assumed it was owned by members of the press pack who, running late and with nowhere else to park, just pitched up behind the goal. After all, back in the 1970s a number of stadiums offered greyhound racing and even speedway, with the track affording plenty of places to park *inside* the ground on matchdays.

More perplexing to us youngsters back in the mid-1970s were the neatly parked rows of cars we saw displayed at matches. Stamford Bridge sticks in the memory, with cars parked neatly in the huge gap between the pitch and the terraces – but why? We can only assume it was the work of some high-powered British Leyland executive, who saw the acres of wasteland behind the goal at the Shed End as an open-air showcase for the formidable Austin Princess. We'd have been more concerned about a wayward Micky Droy clearance smashing a windscreen.

Maybe associating cars with football clubs did wonders for sales? And, from parking cars in the ground it was only a short hop to dealerships sponsoring players to drive their cars. Looking back, the sponsored car was one of the few perks of being a footballer in the 1970s and '80s. Sure, you had to go shopping in a car that had something like 'Alan Mullery drives a Peckham Ford' emblazoned in yellow vinyl on the bonnet – but a free car was a free car, even if it was a Mark II Ford Cortina.

Spotting your local centre-half in his sponsored motor at a pelican crossing was a genuine thrill in the 1970s, and something sadly lacking in the modern game. These days it's all blacked-out windows and armour-plated 4x4s. And the game is a lot worse for it.

Bring back sponsored motors and bring back cars in grounds. And no, the Kassam Stadium car park doesn't count – the cars have to be *inside* the stadium.

Chester-le-Street

As a result of spending too long pawing over pen pictures in the programme (see Pen pictures) or studying our Panini sticker albums, we got in an awful muddle with Brian Robson and Chester-le-Street.

We just couldn't understand it – how come they always listed the actual *street* where Captain Fantastic was born? Everyone else had to make do with a city or a town, or occasionally a county if records were a bit vague. But with Robbo they always listed the street. It confused us for years and it wouldn't go away. In 1982 Robson scored the fastest goal in World Cup history against France and we remember proud residents of Chester-le-Street being interviewed on *World Cup Grandstand* (at least we think we do). Then in '86 he injured his sodding shoulder and Chester-le-Street was back in the news again.

We started to think that Chester-le-Street was the most famous street in Britain. And then the penny dropped. The Romans had called Robbo's birthplace Concangis, but by the Middle Ages it had morphed into Chester in the Strett, then after a bit of interference by some bloke called Norman – and in a bid to distinguish it from the other Chester (near Wales) – they settled on the 'street' bit.

So Robbo was born in a town after all, and the guys at Panini weren't divulging sensitive personal information. As with so much of life, the fantasy was so much better than the reality.

Children of Magic Sponge Mountain

It is hard to believe that a dirty black bucket, water from a questionable source and a stained yellow sponge were integral to the treatment of any football injury – but, for years, this was the only medical help available to both international footballers and park players alike.

The sponge part of this combination was known as 'The Magic Sponge' for its seemingly supernatural powers in fixing players' injuries. The designated physio (usually a symbolic title with no qualifications asked for, or proffered) would sprint on to the pitch and cure injuries from head to toe with a cold, wet sponge. A previously prostrate player would magically spring into life after application, able to continue the match. It was mostly applied to knocks and bruises, but was also used to treat cuts, wounds, twists and, in extreme cases, breaks. Regardless of the severity of the injury players were always instantly cured.

In the heat of matches the sponge could also be used to cool players down or, in some cases, be drunk from. Drinking from a sponge would often directly follow its application to another player's injury. Never more appropriate was Nietzsche's quote: 'That which does not kill us makes us stronger.' The team nutcase would care not that the sponge had just been applied to someone's sweaty bollocks or a bleeding wound, and would theatrically squeeze its contents into his parched mouth regardless.

The sponge worked because players believed in its mystical qualities. Applying cold water to a bruise with a sponge does offer short-term relief, but it is no miracle cure-all. The magic sponge needed us all to believe – and not just to make the injury better, but also to survive the germs that lurked in the depths of that communal black bucket. Is it any coincidence that the world has been plagued by so-called 'super-bugs' since the magic sponge went out of fashion? We're convinced that the frequent transfer of bacteria via a soggy sponge actually boosted our immune systems, making us strong enough to fight off illness. Now, the sponge is history and the very future of the human race hangs in the balance as we fight the latest strain of goat flu.

Not only that, but the EU are left to struggle with a sponge mountain. Butter, Cheese, Sponge? Just how many mountains can these faceless Eurocrats cope with?

Finally, FIFA are constantly struggling to deal with play-ers faking injury. We say bring back the magic sponge and watch the feigning stop overnight – if only because today's pampered players would be desperate to avoid the contents of the murky black bucket.

There you go, in a page of writing we've eradicated 'super-bugs,' got rid of the EU sponge mountain and stopped footballers faking injury. We are here to help, if only someone would listen.

Commercial suicide

We've all done it. Gone for a slash, or nipped out early for a drink or a burger to beat the half-time rush. We've all picked exactly the wrong moment to leave our seats and as a result missed the only noteworthy incident in 90 minutes of pure tedium. It's just one of those things and that's why we can't quite see why everyone is being so hard on ITV.

We are of course referring to the Tic Tac controversy: the moment ITV cut live transmission of Everton v Liverpool in the FA Cup fifth round in 2009, missing the only goal of the game and replacing it with an advert for Tic Tacs – the chirpy sweet that offers 'refreshing little lifts', and all for under two calories a packet (see, we were paying attention).

More than seven million viewers had tuned in to watch the blue and red halves of Merseyside do battle in the FA Cup. Although, we reckon less than 50 of them were still awake after 118 minutes of dirge to actually witness ITV dropping their almighty clanger.

ITV returned to the action just as Everton's Dan Gosling was celebrating his last-gasp winner. The next day everyone was fuming. According to the newspapers, FA supremo Lord Triesman was so outraged he personally telephoned ITV chairman, Michael Grade – initial pleasantries out of the way, we'd like to imagine the line went dead just as he was about to launch into a volley of expletives.

Grade himself went as far as donning a referee's outfit and pretending he was Graham Poll: 'We're still trying to figure out how it happened and there may be a few yellow and red cards following this.' He continued, 'It was a shambles on air. It wasn't deliberate. It wasn't a commercial decision. It was a technical cock-up.'

Of course, the furore did eventually subside. Quick-thinking advertising executives cashed in by releasing an online video recreating the goal with men dressed up as giant yellow and green Tic Tacs (think *It's A Knock Out*, only halve the costume budget). And Evertonians – proving that irony is alive and well on the streets of Merseyside – voted Gosling's strike their goal of the season.

We really don't think it was that bad. As we said at the start, we've all been there (or *not* been there) – we've all missed important goals. And, anyway, anything that makes Steve Rider sweat a little can't be all bad.

Compulsory purchase

This isn't the first time we've ranted about this and it probably won't be the last. We are sick to death of seeing empty seats at the new Wembley Stadium. And we're not talking about the 15 minutes either side of half-time when the luvvies in the posh seats disappear for their champers and nibbles.

No, we are fed up with turning on the telly to see swathes of corporate seats empty for the entire game. It doesn't matter what the occasion, you can guarantee the television cameras will linger on an embarrassingly large number of empty seats – usually those right in line with the centre circle. It could be an important World Cup qualifier; an FA Cup semi-final or the final itself; it doesn't seem to make a difference. You'd half suspect that if England were to host and reach another World Cup final, there would still be empty seats – all because some investment banker called Jeremy decided that he'd rather stay in the country shooting quail than go to the match. If we had our way, it wouldn't be quail being shot.

The FA need to act to stop our nation's showpiece football matches becoming a laughing stock. Any seats left empty for more than one match should be compulsory purchased; and given to kids who could otherwise never dream of affording a ticket to a cup final. Sod the debentures and the ten-year season tickets – fill our national stadium with people who actually care about the result.

Cup final yin-yang

Someone must've read our first book (and we don't just mean the friends and family we held at gun point). In *Modern Football is Rubbish* we sang the praises of football's own Eric & Ernie, yes, *Saint & Greavsie*. We also sadly noted that they'd been confined to TV's scrapheap along with *Metal Mickey*, never to be revived.

Imagine our surprise then, when Setanta announced they were bringing *Saint & Greavsie* back from the televisual wilderness for a 2009 FA Cup final special. It didn't seem possible: Ian St. John and Jimmy Greaves back on our screens after all these years – the shiny suits, the banter, the slightly awkward interviews. Football truly is a funny ol' game.

We've got to admit, it made us feel like the most powerful men in world football. Blatter and Platini had nothing on us; we had single-handedly brought back football's most loved double-act. We were as powerful as Lovejoy in his *Soccer AM* heyday: 'The hardest thing about leaving *Soccer AM* is the thought that I might no longer be influencing the game' – Tim in his bestselling autobiography *Lovejoy on Football*. We'd done it, we were major players. Next up, a proper, sustained, *Roy of the Rovers* revival – as pioneering surgeons we'd sew Roy's famous left foot back on to his leg and before you could say 'near-fatal helicopter accident' his comic would, again, be stuffed through our letterbox every Saturday morning. It would be 1982 all over again, and it would be down to us.

Of course, we were getting ahead of ourselves. But, at the very least, the return of *Saint & Greavsie* was a shot in the arm for the FA Cup. At last, it seemed 'the world's greatest cup competition's' stock was on the rise. If Manchester United's withdrawal in 2000 to take part in the oddball World Club Championship had been the competition's nadir then, nearly ten years on, the revival was complete.

Look at the facts: Saint & Greavsie were back for the FA Cup final – not the Champions League final or the Premiership – but for the competition closest to the nation's heart; the final was established back at Wembley; and after years of those stupid on-the-pitch trophy presentations, the players were back collecting their medals after an arduous ascent to the Royal Box.

With these cup final staples back in place, it was time to work on the finer details. And lo-and-behold, the 2009 final saw the return of even more cup final favourites. Brian Moore used to refer to 'cup final weather', and it did seem that the finals of the 1970s and '80s were always played in blistering heat, causing players to sweat half their body-weight into their heavy polyester shirts, thus bringing on the oft-discussed 'cup final cramp'. The 2009 final was a scorcher, and as a result we got more 'cup final gold' – the cameras zooming in on a pitch-side thermometer showing the temperature had broken the mythical 100-degrees Fahrenheit. We are convinced that every final we watched as kids was played in 100-degree heat. We're pretty sure it was so hot one year Jim Rosenthal successfully fried an egg on the greyhound track that surrounded the Wembley pitch. And it must've been warm 'cos we always came in from our half-time kick-about sweating buckets and demanding a vat of ice-cold Robinson's Barley Water.

The brilliant weather also heralded the return of another cup final oddity – light and shade, or the famous 'Wembley shadow'. We remember the glorious Wembley sunshine playing havoc with the TV coverage, as the cameras struggled to adjust to half the pitch being bathed in sunlight and the other half shrouded in darkness. It is strangely reassuring that – despite the new stadium being rotated through 90 degrees and numerous advances in broadcasting technology that allow us to watch the match in high definition from any number of angles – they still haven't solved the problem of light and shade. We call it cup final yin-yang.

It's nice to see the FA Cup reviving the traditions of our childhood. Giant strides have been made since the late 1990s when the competition seemed in terminal decline. We've got *Saint & Greavsie*, cramp, 100-degree heat and the famous Wembley shadow. All we need now is a bloody underdog to start upsetting the apple cart and winning the competition. We live in hope.

Deal or No Deal

It is becoming increasingly clear that big-money transfers aren't controlled by managers, clubs, or trillionaire chairmen. And they're not even driven by greedy players or unscrupulous agents. They are controlled by Noel Edmonds.

Kaka to Manchester City for £103 million? No deal.

Ronaldo to Real Madrid, £85 million? Deal.

Noel is the transfer daddy – a jovial, bearded front man for The Banker. As for the banker, well, we reckon he's Eric – the oft-referenced but never seen lighting technician from Noel's *Multi-Coloured Swap Shop*. He made his millions flogging second-hand toys in the 1980s and now he's reaping the rewards – and between them Noel and Eric have got the transfer market sewn up.

Dr Football: Own goals count double

Sometimes we take a well-earned break from penning our mix of cutting-edge satire and hate-fuelled polemic. And when we do, we try really hard to think of positive ways to improve the game we love.

This usually involves us swallowing handfuls of Prozac, donning lab coats and safety goggles and descending into Nick's basement to mess about with the Junior Chemistry set he got for Christmas in 1984. The results have been startling – well, ever since we ran out of sulphur and couldn't amuse ourselves making stink bombs. No, our pioneering experiments may just save modern football. So much so that Nick is seriously thinking of changing his name to 'Doctor Football', and retreating permanently to his underground lair, nay, Soccer Lab.*

The first half-arsed idea to emerge from this underground think-tank was to make own goals count double. It works for away goals in certain competitions, so why not extend the remit to own goals? First we imagined the shame a defender would experience knowing that his misplaced backpass had cost his side not one goal but two. Then we laughed – a lot. But the idea was far from perfect, plus it was open to abuse. We didn't mind strikers deliberately trying to cannon shots into defenders in the hope they might skank off them and into the net for a 'double goal'; no, we were more concerned about mysterious betting syndicates corrupting the morals of your average centre-half. So with much sadness, we scrapped the idea.

Our next attempt at blue-sky thinking didn't fare much better either. The central premise behind 'Owen goals counting double' (do you see what we did there? Clever, huh?) was that Michael Owen spends so long on the sidelines injured that every goal he scores deserves to be worth two.

Think of it as a fitting tribute to one of the modern game's greatest strikers – a player whose career has suffered from the twin blows of a niggly hamstring and signing for Newcastle. Still, something wasn't quite right: our blue sky still looked decidedly cloudy.

Then, we cracked it. A fool-proof way of eliminating one of the modern game's major ills. Ask yourself this: after a goal has been scored, is there anything more irritating than another player from the same team smashing the loose ball back into the net – a second time – as part of the goal celebration? It is bloody annoying, especially if the goal is against the team you support and it happens right in front of you. We can't abide the cocky little twits who rub salt into our wounds by boottering the ball back into the empty net.

So here's our plan. It's devilishly simple: if a player from the same side wallops the loose ball back into the net after a team mate has just scored, the goal is instantly disallowed. It is genius. And it would stop this galling practice overnight.

A natural extension of this ruling would see any defender caught bashing the ball back into the net in frustration at conceding a goal penalised by the goal counting double (after all, the ball has hit the back of the net twice).

It's not a bad idea, is it? It's certainly a whole lot better than 'Game 39'.

Obviously, we are not suggesting we introduce this straight away. We suggest trialling it either in Major League Soccer (we're pretty sure zany American 'soccer' fans would go crazy for this sort of shit) or, perhaps, at something relatively low key like the World Cup.

*A routine search on the interweb denotes that there is already a company called Soccerlab. Please do not confuse the two. Ours doesn't really exist.

Dropping anchormen

Forget miners or milkmen. TV anchormen were the unsung heroes of the 1970s and '80s. This select band of swarthy middle-aged gents would spend their Saturday afternoons sweating under the studio lights to bring us goal-flashes from Portman Road or The Hawthorns. These broadcasting stalwarts worked the margins between the latest racing from Kempton (BBC), or bouts of wrestling (ITV), bringing us updates as and when they could decipher the nonsense being fed to them via their primitive earpieces.

Being an anchorman wasn't the multi-media, multi-screen match-fest that today's pampered broadcasters take for granted. No, finding out the score of a game between Carlisle and Peterborough was dependent on some local journo trained in Morse code getting a line out of Cumbria before 4.45pm. That they kept us reasonably abreast of the day's action is even more remarkable when you consider their work was set against the backdrop of industrial action, power cuts and cold war paranoia – was Halifax v Rochdale really 2-2, or was it the Russians feeding us bogus scores in an attempt to undermine the very core of Western democracy?

The anchorman was the public face of an enormous data collection operation that involved hundreds of men and women, banks of telephones, telex machines and the Enigma computer in Bletchley. In the 1970s, more than three-quarters of TV licence-payers' money was spent on bringing us the football scores.

Think back to those Saturdays on the carpet in front of the telly (we sure as hell weren't allowed near the sofa; that was the old man's domain): behind the anchorman, countless minions would scurry to-and-fro clutching bits of paper and scratching their heads. Sometimes what was going on in the background behind Frank Bough was the most interesting bit of *Grandstand* and we'd get quite upset when they cut away to the 4.10 at Newmarket. Collating the football results on a Saturday afternoon didn't just swallow the TV licence fee, it also provided a much-needed boon to the ailing UK labour market. Between 1973 and 1975 one-in-every-two people with a job in Great Britain was employed on *Grandstand*. These days, not even the huge worldwide 'listening' operation directed at Al-Qaeda gets close to the manpower needed to bring us the classified football results.

But our focus is not the behind-the-scenes machinations that brought us *Grandstand* or *World of Sport*; it's the men on the front desk. *Grandstand* was first on the air in 1958 and had rattled through Peter Dimmock, David Coleman and Frank Bough as anchormen by the time we were old enough to fully understand what was going on. And this was half the problem. In 1979, Des Lynam took over the anchor on *Grandstand*, and this meant he was going head-to-head with Dickie Davies on *World of Sport*. We were eight years old and could we tell them apart? No, we couldn't. Both sported impressively lapelled suits, usually in grey or fawn (did they phone each other every Saturday morning to avoid a kit clash?) and opted for a well-maintained moustache (the facial hair of choice for the '70s TV presenter). Most confusingly they both had staggeringly extravagant hair – swept back across their heads – hair that seemed to go a little bit greyer with each passing episode. Eventually we realised that it was Dickie Davies who was pioneering the infamous 'badger streak' (probably to set him apart from Des) – and our dilemma was sorted.

For us, Lynam and Davies represented the pinnacle of the genre. They are the benchmark by which all subsequent anchormen should be judged, and we will probably never have it so good again. *World of Sport* was pulled from our screens in 1985 with Davies still at the helm, while *Grandstand* soldiered on until 2007 fronted by dependable broadcasters including Steve Rider, John Inverdale and Bob

Wilson. But it was never the same. Half Man Half Biscuit documented the demise in song:

> I've been to Kent, Gwent, Senegal
> I've even been to look for Jim Rosenthal
> Found him on his knees at the Wailing Wall crying
> 'Bob Wilson, anchorman'
> *Bob Wilson Anchorman*, Half Man Half Biscuit

As anchormen, Des and Dickie were insurmountable. They kept you glued to the telly through charisma alone. Why else would you spend four hours every Saturday watching a bizarre assortment of horse racing, speedway, darts and wrestling while the sun blazed outside?

These days, satellite broadcasters have nabbed the rights to all the best sports, and as such the anchormen are only found in the televisual hinterland, sandwiched somewhere between the shopping channel and *Dave*. But these rolling sports/news channels may just have offered a lifeline to budding anchormen (and women – hey – it's the 21st century after all!). Despite this upturn in job opportunities, the vast majority of the new generation of anchorpersons end up looking like star-struck estate agents plonked in front of the camera, told to sit up straight and read the autocue. But there is hope. The effervescent Jeff Stelling has been updating satellite viewers on Sky's *Soccer Saturday* since 1994. However, he's really come to prominence since the programme started going out on Freeview.

Jeff is *Soccer Saturday*. A one-man institution that keeps the show going. The more we watch the more we think that he might just be the spiritual heir to Des 'n' Dickie's anchorman empire. He delivers scores, cracks jokes and wrestles with a panel of ex-footballers all out to get one over on him.

True, the BBC's red-button version of Final Score (along with Football Focus, the only things to survive Grandstand's demise) had Ray Stubbs (before he flew the nest) but try as he might, he's no match for Jeff – well, not yet. Just imagine is Stubbsy carves himself an equally impressive niche over at ESPN fronting a rival six-hour result-a-thon?

You see, for all our misty-eyed romanticism for the anchormen of old, we could just be heading into a second golden age. Jeff and Ray may well be the new Des and Dickie – battling it out in a digital ratings war, hoping to win the hearts and minds of the nation's armchair fans. They will have to be in it for the long haul and it might just come down to who can grow the best moustache...

End of season videos killed the radio star

Why did we do it? Why, every year, did we exchange our hard-earned cash for a crumby end of season video?

Rewind to the beginning of the 1980s: Buggles had recently topped the charts with their synthpop classic *Video Killed The Radio Star*. It might've been a throwaway pop record but it was also a chilling portent of what was to happen to football.

For decades match highlights could only be seen on *Match of the Day* or *The Big Match*. Both programmes would restrict themselves to broadcasting three or four games a week – the cost and logistics of outside broadcasting meant anything more was impossible. The sight of a convoy of OB trucks rumbling into town on a Saturday morning only heightened the pre-match tension, as you knew your match was going to be on telly later that night. It was the scarcity of highlights that made them special and, if you were a fan of a lower league club, getting on the telly could be a once-in-a-lifetime experience.

Then came home video. VHS and Betamax arrived in our front rooms and there was only ever going to be one winner – and it wasn't football. Clubs were quick to capitalise, and before we knew what was going on, every kick was being recorded on industrial handycams. The footage was awful: the picture blurry; sound often non-existent; and key-moments were missed with alarming regularity as the cameraman fumbled in his bag looking for a new tape.

Of course, these matches weren't being recorded for posterity; they were being recorded so they could sell us the footage. The end of season highlights video was born, and football would never be the same again. In the early days of home video, you would pay upwards of £20 to watch a badly assembled collection of highlights that bore little resemblance to the matches you were sure you'd watched. Leaving aside the non-existent production values and the fact that the camera lens seemed to be permanently misted over (giving the illusion that the entire season had been played in industrial smog), these videos were rubbish.

There's a Native American superstition that says a photograph or etching of a person steals a part of their soul, and we believe that the same is true of highlights videos. Think of a great match or a dramatic last-gasp winner from the past. Now search out the VHS tape and watch the highlights. Where your memory embellishes and exaggerates the moment, recreating and amplifying the adrenalin rush, the highlights video strips away the emotion, leaving you with a deflected shot, bundled over the line. The fact that this 'momentous' goal was filmed from a distance of half a mile away, through a real peasouper, further devalues the moment.

Then, there's the commentary. In our heads, all commentary duties are contracted to Kenneth Wolstenholme, who magnifies our memories with something profound. In reality, we are saddled with a high-pitched teenager, who fancies himself as the next John Motson, or a delusional local radio reporter with ideas above his station. Five minutes in, and we've hit the mute button, leaving us watching really awful match footage in total silence.

Still, it's not all bad. If there's enough space left on the tape, the producers of the highlights video usually attempt an ambitious audio-visual montage – distilling the entire season into a three-minute pop song. This song was usually *Simply The Best* by Tina Turner. The montage consists of a handful of slo-mo goals and gawky celebrations, again, all filmed from a respectable distance. Turner could probably retire on the PRS revenue from these videos alone (though we doubt that the royalties have ever been paid).

But what really disturbed us wasn't the videos *per se*, it was the fact that we continued to buy them every bloody year. We knew they were shite, yet still we parted with our money. We can only conclude we were desperate football junkies, who lived in hope that a quick VHS-fix would be enough to get us through the close season. Either that, or we naively thought that the videos would improve.

The end of season video didn't kill the radio star, it didn't really kill anyone, but it had the uncanny ability to sting us for twenty quid. We've not watched any, but aside from a flashly menu page, we're pretty sure highlights DVDs are just as crap.

Eric Steele iPod, the

To us, Eric Steele will forever be understudy to Steve Sherwood in the great Watford side of the late 1970s. He didn't play that much, but when he did he never let us down. A distinguished playing career lasting 16 years including successful spells with Newcastle, Peterborough, Brighton and Derby, forever undermined by Nick sticking three-out-of-three penalties past him at a Junior Hornets sports day in 1984.

Little did we know that almost a quarter of a century later Eric Steele would position himself at the forefront of the electronic revolution *and* be the only footballer to have an iPod named after him.

With the 2009 Carling Cup final between Manchester United and Spurs going to a penalty shootout, United goalkeeping coach, Eric Steele, whipped out his iPod and began showing keeper Ben Foster video footage of Spurs players taking penalties. This surprised us quite a bit, as we thought footballers' iPods were only allowed to contain really bad R&B. It seemed to take Foster by surprise as well. He said: 'It had actual video on it and showed where players put things,' adding, 'Eric brought it when he came to the club. I have never seen anything like it. It is a fantastic tool for us.'

This is a great quote on a couple of levels: First, that Foster had never seen *anything* like it – really? Surely someone in the United dressing room has a diamond-encrusted MP3 player? Second, Foster's surprise that it had *actual* video on it leaves us wondering what other kinds of video you can get.

Steele's freethinking earned Apple plenty of free advertising and, as such, we hope they reward him with his own limited edition iPod. If it is good enough for U2 it's good enough for Eric Steele.

It is fair to say that this act of space-age improvisation places Steele alongside the unnamed visionaries who first used a Subbuteo pitch and players as a 3D tactics board, or the bloke who first decided to try and explain the offside rule to his girlfriend using salt and pepper pots.

Apple and Eric – thinking different.

Europa League

So the UEFA Cup is no more, consigned to the dustbin of history where it will slowly rust in a heap alongside the Cup Winners, Mitropa, Zentropa, Latin and various Anglo-Italian Cups.

Of course, the UEFA Cup hasn't actually been scrapped but rebranded for the 2009/10 season as the 'Europa League'. It is not the first time Europe's 'other' cup competition has had a makeover: the UEFA Cup actually began life in 1955 as the clumsily, yet accurately monikered Inter-Cities Fairs Cup. That cup was the brainchild of Sir Stanley Rous among others, and had been set up to promote international trade fairs around Europe. Initially the competition featured representative city sides as well as established teams. The first Fairs Cup took three years to complete and was won by Barcelona, who defeated a London XI 8-2 on aggregate. From 1968 onwards entry to the competition was based on league position, and as such the trophy was often referred to as the 'Runners Up Cup'. English sides were slow starters but by 1971, Leeds (twice), Arsenal and Newcastle (yes, Newcastle) had tasted European glory.

By 1971/72 UEFA, who had regarded the Fairs Cup as something akin to an illegitimate half-brother, took control and with a few tweaks to the rule-book christened it the UEFA Cup – but not before current holders Leeds United and three-times winners Barcelona had competed in a Play-Off to decide who got to keep the Fairs Cup once and for all.

For a while, all was right with the world. Spurs won the first ever UEFA Cup in 1972 with a 3-2 aggregate win over Wolves (see, two English sides in a showpiece European final is nothing new.) The competition, running alongside the Cup Winners Cup and the European Cup, was of great significance with teams throughout Europe desperate to win it. English sides enjoyed considerable success, winning the tournament six times and finishing as runners up on a further four occasions.

Things started to go wrong as UEFA's flagship competition the European Cup morphed into the Champions League. Clubs became increasingly desperate to play Champions League football and came to rely on the money and media coverage it brought with it. The UEFA Cup increasingly became seen as second best, a fact compounded by teams who got knocked out in the qualifying rounds or group stages of the Champions League being parachuted into the UEFA Cup at seemingly random points. In 1999 the once popular Cup Winners Cup was abandoned and national cup winners were absorbed into an increasingly unwieldy UEFA Cup.

To be honest, by the end of the 20th century, no one really knew what was going on with the UEFA Cup. It seemed teams could qualify by any number of bonkers methods: they could finish anywhere from third to seventh in the league and be in with a shout; they could win the FA or League Cup; they could spend all season being really nice to everyone they met and stand a chance of entering through UEFA's fair play lottery; or, if they were really, really keen, teams could volunteer for the Intertoto Cup – a competition that was seemingly designed to give deeply average footballers something to do over the long summer holidays.

The UEFA Cup was a shambles. With so many entrants, preliminary rounds were mixed with round-robin group stages all before the laborious knockout marathon could even begin. Worse than that – clubs stopped taking it seriously. Premier League teams were particularly guilty. It seems ironic that English teams would spend an entire season trying to secure a place in European competition, only to start fielding reserve teams in a crucial tie (hello, Totting-ham, yes, we do mean you). Remind us why you entered in the first place? Was it not the opportunity to win some silverware? A chance to replicate the heroics of Tony Parks *et al* back in '84? Probably, but when push comes to shove Premiership survival far outweighs European glory.

In its most basic terms the demise of the UEFA Cup comes down to cash. It is seen as a second-rate tournament, nowhere near comparable with the Champions League behemoth either in terms of financial reward or prestige – and this is where UEFA's rebranding of the competition as the Europa League seems strangely apt. You see, we just can't shake the image of the *Europa League* as a type of caravan. We know you can see it too. And we're pretty sure we've all been stuck behind one on the M25 at some point.

The Europa League as a caravan is a good metaphor, because no matter how many 'go faster' stripes you stick to the side or how good these new chemical toilets become, a caravan will always be, well, a caravan. In contrast, the Champions League is a glitzy fortnight in Florida with access-all-area passes to Disneyland, MGM Studios, SeaWorld and The Epcot Centre.

So how can the Europa League compete? How can two weeks sharing a caravan in Rhyl compete with a fortnight in the Sunshine State? Well, perhaps the competition should celebrate its differences, not try to ape the appeal of the Champions League. Patrick Barclay, the Chief Football Commentator of *The Times*, hit the nail on the head when he said that the competition needs to go back to basics – back to its '70s heyday. The UEFA Cup/Europa League needs to go back to a straight knockout format. We agree with Barclay that it should be reinvented as a kind of pan-European FA Cup. Every game would mean something: scrap the seeding system and genuine cup upsets would never be far away. It would add genuine drama and excitement to the second tier of European competition.

Reverting to a traditional knockout competition solves half the problem. But how do we persuade clubs to take the tournament seriously and field full-strength sides? It isn't going to be easy, and sadly the only way to achieve this would be to throw money at it. Perhaps some of the prize money from the Champions League pot could be diverted in its direction? Make the competition worth winning and, perhaps, some of these once proud clubs will start to take it seriously. There's a certain irony that a competition that was brought into being by a need to promote commerce now needs a shot in the arm from commerce to keep it alive.

For us, it should be enough to want to win every game you play, but for Europe's not-so-elite, this isn't always the case. So, why not dangle a financial carrot, especially if it means saving this once proud caravan – sorry – competition.

Failing that, next time you are stuck on the M25 behind a slow moving *Europa League*, give 'em a cheery toot – they are probably on their way to Belgium to watch Club Brugge against Nancy.

Famous five-a-side

When we first put pen to paper writing *Modern Football is Rubbish*, we would dream. We'd dream about outselling JK Rowling. We'd dream about becoming the new *Baddiel & Skinner* – penning a World Cup anthem, and hosting our own irreverent football chat show. We'd dream that our words of wisdom would kick-start a revolution – a revolution that would save football from itself. But more than anything, we'd dream about playing in celebrity five-a-side tournaments.

We'd watch Ant & Dec's *Soccer Aid* or read about Sky's *The Match* and dream of being asked to get involved. You could keep the other trappings of fame and celebrity – for years we thought China White was a colour in B&Q's home-brand paint collection, not a trendy nightspot favoured by footballers – but give us the opportunity to be chastened by Graham Taylor, 'Demand it Nico, demand it!' – and we'd bite your arm off. All we really wanted was to sell enough copies of our book to be invited to play football with the stars of screen and stage.

That's not to say our intentions were entirely honourable. We'd sit watching Angus Deayton strut around Old Trafford and think how nice it would be to get properly stuck in. You see, it might be for charity, but we'd bet the viewing public would dig just that little bit deeper to see their 'favourite' celebrities being clattered, two-footed from behind. The trouble with these showbiz matches is that everyone is so nicey-nicey – they never know when they'll next be thrown together in the Green Room of some Saturday night chat show, and, as a result, the match would pass off like a particularly lame pre-season friendly.

These days, we're under no illusion that we'll ever make it to the big time and, as such, our football dreams remain just that. But all this has done is make our dreams darker and even more twisted. We frequently find ourselves mulling over our ultimate, fantasy five-a-side opponents – it's enormous fun; you should try it.

There are only two celebrity criteria: first, they should really get on your tits; second, they should have a tenuous connection to football. After all, it is too easy just to include Gordon Brown or David Cameron just because you can't stand their politics.

So here's the line-up of celebrities we'd like to go head-to-head with on the Astroturf (most of them have been mentioned elsewhere in this book, so their inclusion shouldn't come as too much of a surprise):

Eamonn Holmes (he'd be the goalie, right?)
Jeremy Clarkson
Angus Deayton
Tim Lovejoy
Gordon Ramsay
Sub: Alistair Campbell

As celebrity fantasies go, it's right up there with the one we keep having about us, Ulrika and the woman who used to be the roving reporter for Setanta. Just imagine lining up against that lot at five-a-side – Holmes, Clarkson, Deayton, Lovejoy, Ramsay, Campbell – it would be Christmas come early. And no, lads, slide-tackles *aren't* banned. We'd be prepared to suffer for weeks from those weeping sores you get when you slide in on Astroturf, just for the opportunity to execute a perfectly timed tackle on Lovejoy. Make no mistake, this would be no celebrity love-in, this would be proper blood and thunder football.

Come on Channel 4, you are quite happy to put celebs through the mill for weeks on end in the *Celebrity Big Brother* house, so how about an hour on the Astroturf? *Famous-Five-A-Side* – we've even gifted you the title. Just make sure you invite us to the party.

Faux-centenaries

The thing is with centenaries – they only come around every 100 years. When they're gone, they're gone, and all you can do is sit patiently and wait for the next one (a bit like waiting for a train on the Northern Line after about 10pm on a Sunday). Except, ever-ingenious football club marketing departments are seemingly able to dream up new reasons to celebrate/rip-off supporters at the drop of a hat.

How about celebrating our 110-year anniversary? Great idea. What about 75 years of playing in a particular stadium (despite all of the ground's original, redeeming features being replaced by four identikit concrete stands in 1997)? Brilliant. Twenty-five-years since we appeared in the semi-finals of the Anglo-Italian cup? Let's produce commemorative home and away kits to celebrate.

It's getting stupid. We are all for commemorating historic events – hell, nostalgia is the oxygen we breathe – but these faux-centenary celebrations just feel like a rip-off, an excuse to fleece the fans by producing cheap merchandise.

How do we stop this ridiculous debasing of genuine history? We dock points, that's what we do. Any club caught churning out tawdry tat commemorating 20 years of winning the Milk Cup or reaching the Northern final of the Leyland DAF trophy, dock 'em points – that, as Francis Fukuyama would say, will be the end of faux-history.

Fifteen seconds of fame

We are getting sick of turning on the telly to watch the football, only to be greeted by two gurning faces, jumping up and down, hugging each other, howling as if they've just won the lottery and waving back at us. Sorry, do we know you?

We're not talking about Premiership prima donnas over-celebrating a two-yard tap-in. And we're not talking about two FA stooges getting all worked up over the draw for the FA Cup fifth round.

No, we are talking about the fans. The ones picked out by the cameraman as he waits for the teams to re-emerge from the tunnel after the half-time break. You know exactly how it unfolds... The cameraman pans slowly round the stadium before zooming in on a couple of fans idly chatting – if this is a World Cup and the cameraman/producer/director is some swarthy over-sexed continental in his early 40s, then these two fans *will* be attractive females in cropped-replica shirts and little flags of Brazil or Sweden in face paint on either cheek (probably some directive issued from the summit of Mount FIFA by Lord Sepp) – anyway, we digress... for a couple of blissful seconds the fans in question are oblivious to their appearance on the telly, then they glance up at the big screen – and start celebrating like banshees.

Congratulations, you are on the telly, and you didn't have to queue for hours in the rain to audition for *Britain's Got Talent*. Oh, hang on, here comes Phil Dowd, looks like the second half is about to get underway.

The only thing worse than this Warhol-*lite*, 15 seconds of jumbo-sized fame, is the big screen showing pictures of kids in floods of tears at the end of a match. This isn't the kids' fault – football is an emotional business and we certainly spent most of our childhood sobbing – it is down to telly executives desperately trying to bag the one 'shot' that encapsulates the mood of desolation. This is just about acceptable when we are dealing with a dramatic last day-of-the-season relegation or a shock World Cup penalty exit, but a 1-1 draw at home to Middlesbrough – in September?

So, telly companies, knock it on the head. How about a nice picture of a seagull on the roof of the stand, or the sun setting over the away end? Anything but the inane gurning and waving.

Football killed The Man from Del Monte

Before isotonic energy drinks, bananas and Jaffa Cakes took over the lucrative half-time snack market, oranges ruled the world. Kids and adults alike grappled with the citrus fruit to replace whatever it was that oranges replaced when they arrived for the half-time team talk. The oranges were frequently delivered on a plate, already cut in half by the manager's wife or that week's designated orange provider.

Hands grabbed at segments of orange – the only option if you wanted your thirst quenched. If you were really posh your mum might have sent you with a bottle of water in an old plastic cordial bottle, but that was showing off. In those days elderly female family members were the only people allowed to administer Lucozade, and only then if you were critically ill. Back in the austere 1970s Lucozade was considered beyond the reach of the average family and never made it as a football staple, and as a result, the mighty orange remained the half-time refreshment of choice.

Not everyone liked oranges, but there was no alternative offered or expected. Greedy players often had two, while other players went empty-handed. It wasn't an exact science and there was often only just enough to go round.

There was one unfortunate side effect of having oranges at half-time – sticky finger syndrome. Holding the orange with both hands, and then sucking out the juice, inevitably meant that some of the juice ended up on your hands. Pitches had no running water facilities, so what could you do with your hands? The first option was wipe them on your shirt. This wiped off some of the juice, but your hands were still sticky. The second option was to spit on your hands. This could work, but it was not easy to raise a spit when the only fluid you had taken on was 10ml of orange juice. The final option was not one for the faint-hearted: should you need to go to the toilet, your pee could be used to good effect.

The raising of living standards in the early '90s and cheaper availability of snacks led to the demise of the orange as a half-time force. An oft-mimicked John Barnes-inspired Lucozade advert encouraged many amateurs to bring their own drinks to matches. The ready availability of energy drinks and advice from all areas of the media about the importance of drinks as an aid to performance meant that personal responsibility for half-time refreshment became the norm. No longer were drinks only hurled from the touchline at sun-drenched World Cup matches. Players up and down the country were taking every opportunity to down volumes of liquid. Breaks in play for injuries or substitutions would enable footballers to hastily head for the bench and grab a bottle. As is often the way, this trend was soon imitated in the parks and pitches of Britain.

Of course, there were losers as a result of this seismic shift in half-time refreshment. The local greengrocer is the obvious one. We do not have figures, but Saturday morning sales must have dipped, substantially. Then, there must have been an EU orange mountain housed somewhere in southern Europe (Seville, in all probability). Imagine a huge warehouse bursting at the seams with over-ripe oranges, then imagine some poor work experience lad opening the door and letting them all spill out – sticky.

No one knew about '5-a-day' when the Premier League started, but another fruit was starting to appear in a footballer's diet. Already popular in tennis, the banana made a bid for the orange's crown.

Gordon Strachan was one footballer who spoke enthusiastically about the value of bananas as Leeds won the title in 1992. Suddenly bananas were everywhere and the orange had lost vital ground that it would never, ever regain. Bananas fought with Jaffa Cakes and Lucozade as the new super-food for football.

By far the biggest casualty in the demise of the orange was The Man from Del Monte. He rode into villages to taste-test oranges to see if they were up to the Del Monte standard, before an excited Spaniard shouted, 'The man from Del Monte, eee say yessssssss!'

Everyone in the village then proceeded to cheer or throw their hats in the air. He wore a white suit and white fedora-style hat; Del Monte's answer to Malcolm Allison, if you like. He was old and Grandpa-like, but he made people happy on a daily basis.

With his fruit in high demand across the football world, the orange was king of all fruits and The Man from Del Monte was a cultural icon. The catch phrase spread across Britain, but the man himself never actually said anything, happy to keep a dignified silence and give the camera a knowing, slightly smug look.

But The Man from Del Monte disappeared from our screens almost as soon as football kicked the orange into touch. True, The Man from Del Monte was actually promoting his own brand of orange juice, but the fallout from the demise of the half-time orange must've played a part in the adverts being pulled from the telly (anyway, cut us a little poetic licence, we've come this far and we really like the mental image).

Brian Jackson, the English actor who played him, was left kicking his heels as the Premier League signed deals with a host of snack food and energy drink conglomerates. Oh, for a club to adopt him as their mascot and give the great man another shot at stardom.

If we've learnt anything from the demise of The Man from Del Monte it is that the impact football has on all aspects of society cannot be overlooked. The ongoing success of football as a global brand has changed many habits, some for better, but most for worse. The withdrawal of The Man from Del Monte from our TV screens was definitely a change for the worse.

Of course, we're pretty sure that Del Monte Foods would argue that The Man from Del Monte's demise was nothing to do with football and everything to do with wanting to advertise their product in a different, more contemporary way. We might beg to differ, but in the end all we can do is say, 'Yesssss.'

Forgotten pains of football
No.1: the grass burn

The long, hot nights that occasionally engulfed Britain in summer were hard to combat at the best of times. But there was one football injury that made those sweaty summer nights even more painful: the grass burn.

In the hot weather football pitches became very hard, very quickly. Penalty areas became dust bowls while the rest of the pitch set as hard as concrete. On top of all this, the inevitable hosepipe ban meant the watering of the playing surface was never an option.

Growing up in the 1970s, ridiculously short shorts were the *only* option in the summer months. The winter haberdashery of Wellington boots and jeans topped off with a parka were exchanged for Woolies' shorts and football tops. Football filled our summer holidays, and regardless of the weather the pace didn't slow. Players could catch a breather if the ball got booted over a hedge but in general matches were just as frenetic as in the winter months.

Tactics certainly didn't change to combat the intense heat and bone-dry pitches. The slide-tackle remained the challenge of choice. In winter, you could gracefully glide through the mud to execute a last-ditch tackle, but in the height of summer the outcome was startlingly different. Yes, the slide-tackle could still be made, but the tight-fitting shorts rode up your leg as the challenge went in, exposing a fleshy thigh.

There was only one result: the dreaded grass burn. Green streaks of grass would mingle with painful red skid-marks as spots of blood began to seep to the surface where the skin had been broken. It hurt, but a grass burn was no reason to stop playing. In fact, you would wear it as a badge of honour for the duration of the game. And, although the injury would put some players off attempting the slide again, as a true footballer – prepared to do anything for your team – you would complete the same manoeuvre again and again, ripping your thigh to shreds.

At first, the adrenalin rush of playing football would mask the pain, but this would slowly give way to a constant stinging sensation. Sitting upright on a chair was just about bearable, but real problems came at the end of a day when a bath had to be taken following eight hours of playing football in 80-degree heat. Broken skin and hot water is a potent combination. Following the bath and the realisation that the grass burn was actually quite painful, came a moment of pure torture. Your Mum would insist on dabbing the wound with cotton wool *soaked* in TCP. Make no mistake, this stung and left you in a whimpering heap on the bathroom floor.

What followed was a hot, delirious, sweaty night. The only option was to lie on your front or back. Even then the pyjamas stuck to the weeping mess on your legs. If you managed to fall asleep and rolled over on to your raw thigh, the cloth of your pyjamas required a quick and painful tug from your skin. In the heat of the night sweat dripped into your wound. Sleep was impossible and this was when the delirium kicked in. You'd wrestle with the bedclothes, desperately changing positions. You'd curse your impetuosity earlier in the day – but there was no escape. The grass burn had won the battle, and you no longer revelled in your toughness.

The grass burns of your youth were all very well, but to achieve cult status amongst the slide-tackle community you have to commit the slide on an indoor pitch, concrete surface or an early version of astroturf.

An indoor pitch actually helps you skid, and creates a less bloody, but longer-lasting burn. Concrete provides a similar effect, but an uneven surface can increase the blood factor. The acid test is a slide-tackle made on the early incarnations of astoturf (which bears no resemblance to the grass-inspired turf you can find at 5-a-side centres like *Goals*). Early Astroturf was exactly the same as the stuff you used to find on display in greengrocers. The 'grass' itself was bad enough, but a liberal sprinkling of sand was added to all early astro-pitches, so that when you slid the sand would multiply the friction. Even Luton's plastic pitch was similar – and that was for professionals. A slide-tackle on this surface didn't burn or graze, it simply removed your skin. As you rolled round in agony the fine sand gathered in your wound, often becoming embedded in your body forever, too painful to extract. Covered or exposed, this injury left you scars which took years to fade. Arms, knees and thighs were all at risk. We know only too well; we still have the scars.

Today's footballers have it easy. Watered pitches, next-generation astroturf that even smells like grass and, of course, longer shorts. Where did it all go wrong?

Forgotten pains of football
No.2: the stitch

The stitch or 'poor man's cramp' attacks not long after eating. You would have thought we would have realised this as youngsters, but no. We continued to race back down to the park straight after tea, only to be hit by the silent assassin. All this despite our parents' desperate refrains of 'Let your tea go down.' How we wished we'd listened.

Like cramp, the first time you get a stitch, you think you are going to die. A stitch has the power to stop you in your tracks and cause your body to contort in ways you didn't think possible. Clutching your side in a theatrical manner was an essential response to the acute stabbing pain. In fact it was the only response.

But providing you survived that first attack, you knew that the pain was temporary. The best feeling in the world was to be hit by a stitch in the middle of a mazy run, clutch your side, yell in agony 'STITCH', pause for a moment then continue your run and slot the ball past the keeper. Up yours, stitch!

Kids spent large chunks of the 1970s running round their local rec holding their sides. Well, the tough ones did anyway. The weak just stood around bent double, moaning. Then, as suddenly as it arrived, it slipped away, a bit like your favourite uncle at Christmas.

There was one thing we didn't understand though: the stitch never attacked the fat kids. Was it scared, or did it have a healthy respect for them? We are not sure.

Forgotten smells of football
No.1: dubbin

Dubbin is, perhaps, football's true forgotten smell. Ask around: no one will remember exactly what it smelled of, but they'll all say it smelled of something.

To us, dubbin smells of damp autumn afternoons; of grass stains and old newspaper; set against a backdrop of a Sunday roast. You see, back in the 1970s, applying dubbin to your newly purchased football boots was the law.

Dubbin was a sort of clear, waxy shoe-polish. By applying it to your newly purchased football boots (bought from a high-street sports shop if you were posh, or from Woolies if you weren't) your boots became impermeable to water. It was the same dubbin with which they used to coat World War Two submarines – it was awesome.

We always forgot to apply the dubbin before we debuted our new Gola boots, but our mums weren't going to let us off the hook that easily. So every September, after the first game of the new season, we'd go through the same routine. Home from the match, quick bath, then downstairs to scrape the mud off our boots. Once they were spick and span, Mum would produce the dubbin and we'd set about applying this strange substance, not being entirely sure it wasn't just our old man's Brylcreem in a different tin. Then, once the dubbin had been properly worked into the leather with an old brush, and after we'd given them a final going over with a J-cloth, we'd stuff newspaper into the toes of our boots and leave them under the radiator to dry. We knew the radiator bit wasn't right, we'd all heard the playground horror stories of brand new boots shrinking two sizes, but we really didn't care, we wanted results – and fast.

So, before our tea was on the table, we'd cleaned our boots and coated them in a substance designed to survive the impending nuclear apocalypse. Our boots were invincible

– and by the same token, so were we (obviously, all that reading of 'Billy's Boots' in *Roy of the Rovers* had left us with deep psychological issues). Only that was it. After that first Sunday of the season had been and gone, we did precisely nothing to look after our boots. We just left them festooned with mud in a grimy Tesco carrier bag at the bottom of our sports holdall. We're not sure if it was due to an insane confidence in the chemical properties of dubbin, or just sheer laziness. The smart money's on the latter.

It is also worth noting that dubbin shouldn't be confused with linseed oil. In 1981, Shaun, still giddy from a summer of applying layer after layer of linseed oil to his cricket bat and inspired by Beefy Botham's ability to switch seamlessly between the worlds of cricket* and football, thought it would be a good idea to add a coating of linseed to his new footy boots. Apparently, the results were spectacular – really bringing out the grain in the leather, but never quite drying.

So there you have it: we can't quite remember what dubbin smelt like, but we know from bitter experience not to confuse it with linseed oil.

* We appreciate this is a book about football, and most of the time we hold all other sports in complete contempt, but all this talk of dubbin and linseed oil got us thinking: every (non-World Cup) year in June we'd take a week or two's break from booting the football around the garden and take up cricket. This has left us pondering a couple of very important issues. First, why did we spend £1.99 on a cheap cricket bat and £3.99 on a tin of linseed oil? Then, after a couple of days slogging a tennis ball around the local park, why did our cricket bat always split in the same spectacular fashion? You know exactly how it happened: you'd lunge at an inviting chest-high bouncer hoping to smack the ball out of the park and into the graveyard next door, but you'd miss the ball completely, only to see the main bit of your bat go flying towards some poor sod standing at silly mid-off. You'd be stood there like a lemon gripping the handle and that pointy triangle of wood that got left behind – and that was the end of cricket for another year.

Forgotten smells of football
No.2: onions

Smells that remind you of *playing* football abound: a whiff of embrocation, creosote, dubbin, even freshly cut grass and we are instantly transported back to the playing fields of our youth. Smells that remind us of going to a match are another matter entirely.

The definitive 'spectator' smell probably hinges on exactly when and where you started watching your football. If you were first taken to the match in the 1920s or '30s, the smell would have been Woodbines. Between the wars, you were only allowed in the ground if you were in possession of a full packet of fags – children as young as eight were known to smoke 60 or more cigarettes during particularly tense cup-ties.

By the 1960s smells had moved on. A curious mixture of stale beer, Bovril and flatulence was the order of the day in most grounds, but as the decade got into full swing, the sweet smell of marijuana, opium and revolution lingered in the air on the bohemian terraces of West London.

The 1970s terrace smelt mostly of Brut and Old Spice; the 1980s smelt of piss; the '90s of uncertainty, a smell that was quickly superseded by 'the noughties', and the unmistakable stench of money, which hung heavy in the air, as real fans were squeezed out by the corporates.

But before we descend into a downward spiral of cynicism, there is one smell that we've yet to mention – one smell to rule them all. And that smell is: onions.

Close your eyes, inhale deeply and think of onions. We guarantee you see yourself in a busy crowd making your way to or from the match. You catch a whiff of something in the air – it is the unmistakable smell of onions frying.

The smell would drift across the crowd from a burger van or mobile cart, tricking your senses, making you feel an incredible hunger that could only be satiated by a ridiculously overpriced burger or hot dog. It wasn't the meat products you really wanted – it was the onions. The smell of them sizzling on an industrial skillet was impossible to resist. Then, there was the pleasure of the squeezy bottles filled with red and brown sauce. After your purchase, you were free to apply as much sauce to your burger as humanly possible. Only the stupid would limit themselves to one type of sauce; both red and brown were the order of the day. Oh, and mustard if it was available (we say mustard; we really mean 'yellow' sauce, as we're pretty sure no actual mustard was used in the production process). The more we think about it, the more we realise that the actual 'meat' product was just an excuse – something on which to hang our delicious mixture of fried onions and rainbow sauces.

It didn't matter when we succumbed – on the way in or out of the ground – a burger with onions and lashings of red, brown and yellow sauce was an integral part of our matchday ritual. And it was always the unforgettable smell of frying onions that lured us in.

Games you couldn't make up No.1: balloon football

This is a curious game: playable only after special occasions, and involving any number of players depending on the size of your living room.

Family gatherings inevitably involved balloons. Not the helium-filled foil types you see these days, but plain, air-blown balloons. Vast numbers built up in the hours leading up to the house party, but were sadly neglected once festivities died down. Usually found in a humorous cock and balls triumvirate in the corners of the room where the ceiling meets the wall, they eventually found their way into the welcoming hands of us kids (blissfully unaware of the fact they'd been arranged in phallic fashion) when gravity won out and the sticky-tape allowed them to fly to freedom.

The beauty of the balloon as a football was its silence. While adults slept off the effects of alcohol, or joyfully widened family rifts, children went about creating fantasy games, with oblivious adults just feet away – at least that's what we did. The obvious goals were door frames. Most rooms have two, so it didn't take much imagination to conjure up a pitch between them. With obstacles plentiful, you could imagine Stuart Hall howling with delight as an eight-year-old kid is once again tackled by the television stand.

The balloon could be kicked as hard as you like towards the goal, swerving in all directions, without worry of damage. Although, as we frantically attempted to score there was always a lull as the balloon slowly floated to a level low enough for us to attempt a header or kick. Overhead kicks and scissor kicks were executed after a flying jump from the sofa. Despite the small playing area, goals were rare as the balloon rarely hit the door due to a sudden uplift of air brought about by the goalie's desperate lunge.

In balloon football, taller players had a distinct advantage as they could attack the ball before it came into smaller players' range, so – for the younger, shorter sibling – the shirt pull was a legitimate, levelling tactic.

If no siblings were available, balloon football could also be a solo pursuit: the balloon was bustled toward each door, and when within a certain area a shot was taken. The same player then attempted to save his own shot, acting as the opposition goalie. It may not sound like fun, but add a running commentary and suddenly it was like playing at Wembley. Played indoors at a hectic pace, the game often ended up with the participants stripped down to pants and vests. At New Year, with the party running into the small hours and the Economy 7 heating kicking in to combat the cold, it was sometimes possible to recreate the exact conditions experienced by Bobby Charlton *et al* at Mexico '70 – the condensation would drip from the windows and you would be sweating – quite literally – for England.

Unfortunately, in balloon football, the potential for injury was high. The most common injury involved stubbing your toe on furniture. This was the cause of Shaun's worst ever football injury – a broken little toe. He was 18.

That's what we did to occupy ourselves 20 years ago. So why not spread a little magic this Christmas and blow up some balloons?

Games you couldn't make up No.2: it's just not cricket

Not so much a game, more a terrorist attack and here's the reason why...

The average council football pitch is generally unprotected. Anyone can play in the goal area at any time, hence the huge crater the goalie stands in, unable to reach the crossbar. A proper goal is rarely unoccupied. Even during half-time in your average Sunday League game kids will take over the goal for a quick game of three-and-in. No one gives a stuff. It's all part of football's rich tapestry – it's a game for the people and everyone should be allowed to join in.

Yet one part of the municipal sports ground remains fenced off for half the year, seemingly holy, sacrosanct and not for the likes of us oikish footballers – it's the cricket strips. Usually, rope dangled between metal poles is the only barrier stopping anyone from entering and, for the most part, people respect this sanction. But this is where the hi-jinks start – what is the protocol when the inevitable happens and the ball from your match strays into the roped-off area?

Usually supporters, not wearing dangerous football boots, will cautiously tip-toe into the demilitarised zone and retrieve the ball. But then there's always the burly fan who attempts to hurdle the rope. A schoolboy error that we urge you not to repeat. Arms and legs go everywhere, grass and mud stains abound. The ego has crash-landed. Priceless.

Then, there's gamesmanship. A ball booted into the out-of-bounds cricket square is the perfect time-wasting tactic. This adds a new dimension to the relevance of the cricket strips. It's a weapon that you know the greatest managers would exploit, if they only had the chance.

With the ball resting slap-bang in the middle of the cricket square, the team in the lead are more than happy to leave the ball for a spectator or lino to retrieve, while the losing team are happy to throw protocol and etiquette out of the window and race onto the sacred turf – *in studs!* Despite shouts from concerned spectators, the vandalism continues until the ball is returned to its spiritual home – on the other side of the flimsy security cordon.

There are two points we must raise. First, if cricketers do not want footballers to 'redress the balance between bat and ball', do not put the cricket square so tantalisingly close. Second, the added attraction of upsetting rival sports is not central to the game of football, but provides a hugely enjoyable distraction for young and old.

PS: Don't ever get us started on bowling greens – all that perfectly flat, beautifully manicured green grass, it's just crying out for a game of five-a-side.

Games you couldn't make up No.3: roofball

As you may be beginning to realise, the number of football related games we made up were almost limitless. Many of these games helped our skills without us even realising it. Games that deviated from regular football were often fraught with danger, but this only added to their appeal.

One such game was roofball. The basic premise was that you had to boot the football over the roof of your house on the volley, with the ball thrown from your hands like a goalkeeper. This may not seem hard, but when you are only eight it's a pretty tricky task.

Danger came in a number of forms: the biggest and most obvious problem was that the ball could get stuck on the roof and that would be the end of that – unless someone fancied risking life and limb to retrieve the ball.

Generally you would kick the ball over the house to mates or siblings who would monitor where it landed or would attempt to catch it. Of course, the other major problem was that the ball was equally likely to land in next door's garden, or somewhere inaccessible, like up a tree. A variation on a theme was to have a load of kids start in the same position as the kicker and then race round the back of the house trying to get to the ball first. The potential for a pile-up was enormous and minor injury a regular occurrence.

The size of your house also affected the game. We used to be content in the knowledge that rich bastards in a mansion would never discover the pleasure of this simple pursuit. On the flipside, bungalow dwellers had a distinct advantage, but not so much fun (but, let's face it, it was only your grandparents that lived in bungalows, so it didn't really matter).

The road was a potentially lethal hazard. The danger didn't arise from running into the road to get the ball, but came from irate drivers who didn't appreciate a dent in their bonnet.

How did roofball help us? Well, volleying was an important technique, as was kicking over distance – especially if you were a goalie or a member of the 'Crazy Gang'. But, above all, roofball allowed us to use our imaginations. It was fun and killed more than a few hours at the weekend.

Games you couldn't make up No.4: stairball

Ideal for the solo player, especially those with small or non-existent gardens. It was the indoor sport of choice for the only child, the only requirements being a ball and a set of stairs.

The player stood at the bottom of the stairs, preferably with a door behind him acting as his goal. The game started when the ball was flicked up onto the stairs – we say ball, but quite often, due to the indoor nature of the game, rolled-up socks were used instead as a sop to damage limitation (see below). A goal was scored when the ball reached the top of the stairs. A goal was scored for the (invisible) opposition if it hit the door behind the player. There were often long periods between goals, as the player successfully defended his goal.

The ball would bounce back down the stairs at all angles and speeds, making it particularly difficult to control. It was a great way of improving reactions, and practising clearances of balls at different heights and speeds. A degree of control and thought had to be exercised, otherwise the ball would come careering back down the stairs at you at impossible speed. Stairball wasn't just a game of skill and speed, it was a game of tactics and intelligence – a bit like chess, only with rolled-up socks and stairs.

There were drawbacks, of course. Obviously, there was a high risk of damage to internal fixtures and fittings. Industry recommendation was the removal of all breakable objects, which was not always easy. Pictures on stairway walls were particularly unhelpful, as was a window at the top of the stairs.

Although not really a spectator sport, there were occasionally freak injuries to those innocent inhabitants who wandered unsuspectingly onto the field of play. Noise complaints were also an unwelcome distraction if the stairway was situated next to the lounge. However, these were small prices to pay for the right to hone your football skills.

Given the wet weather that Britain endured for most of the 1970s, the unholy trinity of hall, stairs and landing was frequently the only place available to practise. Before computer games enabled kids to play as their heroes without a real football, stairball was a cheap, albeit high-risk, alternative. We urge kids today to kick-start stairball again. Who knows, with a groundswell of popular support it might make it all the way to the 2012 Olympics?

Gardening leave

The rise of new terminology in football continues unabated. The innocent-sounding 'gardening leave' is one such phrase that has crept into the game at its highest levels. While footballers are suspended or fined for misconduct, any manager or high-ranking club official is immediately reported as being on 'gardening leave'.

A footballer can be sent off for two rash tackles while trying to maintain his club's league status, and he is banned for a couple of games and fined a few quid. At managerial level, anything from a dodgy comment to fraudulent behaviour results in gardening leave. This seems to involve kicking your heels at home waiting to leave your old club and receiving a huge payout as a thank you for your disloyalty. Usually a juicy contract from a new club has already been signed. And while the two clubs try to reach an agreement the central party is a winner on every level.

But, here's the problem: it's impossible to imagine some of the officials involved actually getting down and dirty in the garden. We imagine them watching a hired-hand completing their gardening as they drink Pimm's, in a deckchair, wearing a straw boater.

We need to make gardening leave a more worthy sentence. Alan Titchmarsh should be sent round to check on the standard of the labours undertaken. A medal could then be issued, much like the ones they hand out at the Chelsea Flower Show. The quality of horticulture should directly affect the payout from the current club, and the future salary of the official in question. Titchmarsh would become a Football Gardening Czar, and sit at Sir Trevor's right-hand side.

Gardening leave should involve actual gardening. The FA should make it mandatory. There's nothing we'd enjoy more than seeing certain high-profile football officials knee-deep in horse manure, shovelling shit for their very future.

Geordie Messiahs

Much has been made of Geordies and their Messiah complex. First Keegan, then Shearer – both played cameo roles in Newcastle's relegation from the Premier League.

Villa fans hit the nail on the head with their cheeky banner on the final game of the 2008/09 season: 'Who's your next Messiah, Ant or Dec?' Personally, we'd go for the dream-combo of Ant, Dec and Jimmy Nail. Failing that, we'd give Jayne Middlemiss a go.

And Gazza? No, he's not the Messiah – he's a very naughty boy.

Getting the Goldie Horn

Before Henry, there was Cantona, before Cantona there was Six, but before them all came Henri Tremont. Henri who, you ask? Well, back in 1980, he was the envy of men across the globe – and he played football!

It was a full year before *Escape to Victory* and two years before *Gregory's Girl*. Football did not translate well to the big screen and obsessed fans had to search long and hard for any football connections at the movies. A hint of footy instantly made films more attractive to most adolescent males, although the actresses involved would soon supersede this.

This football cameo was a gem, although a football was not part of the scene. *Private Benjamin* was pure Hollywood, but Goldie Hawn's love interest was French. In what was footballing fantasy for men everywhere, following a night of passion, Henri left Judy Benjamin to play football with his mates: hurriedly putting his football kit on with his friends waiting, and stepping in dog's piss in the process. He even had the audacity to snatch a kiss as he left.

The scene highlighted the camaraderie that football generates between blokes and hints at the wider social implications of leaving the partner home alone. It was only a very short scene, but it encapsulated the allure of football perfectly.

How many men have been encouraged to undertake one form of physical activity while dreaming of the other? Thank you, Henri. Goldie, we can only apologise.

Goal-kicks for centres

'Goal-kicks for centres' is a lesser-known cousin of 'jumpers for goalposts'. But, mark our words, it is only a matter of time before *The Fast Show's* Ron Manager is caught on camera muttering, 'Goal-kicks for centres. Isn't it? Mmmmmm. Marvellous.'

'Goal-kicks for centres' was a playground staple from our childhood. With the sides picked, the goalkeeping situation resolved (see Rush, Stick or Scramble), the only thing left to confirm prior to getting underway was that goal-kicks were replacing centres – essentially, rather than hoiking the ball back to the centre-spot after a goal, play was allowed to resume from the keeper's kick. It wasn't rocket science, but it was essential that the issue was resolved before the game commenced – if it wasn't agreed then the team who scored first would be in the middle of some elaborate goal-celebration only to find that their opponents had run the length of the pitch unchallenged and slotted home the equaliser. This would cause a right furore and the distinct possibility of the match being abandoned in favour of a bit of a bundle.

The more we think about our football experiences, the more we realise that 'goal-kicks for centres' was pretty much ubiquitous. From the playground to the rec, via five-a-side matches the nation over, 'goal-kicks for centres' was the order of the day – and still is. In fact, it's only proper 11-a-side matches that persist with returning the ball to the centre spot. Perhaps the powers that be should consider giving in to popular opinion – it could be as revolutionary as scrapping the backpass or allowing referees to dress in fuchsia.

'Goal-kicks for centres. In the Premier League? Mmmmmm. Marvellous.'

Goalie's golden rule

Goalie's golden rule... always get the bloody ball!

That was the law of park games when we were growing up. The rationale behind it was that the goalie had an easy time of it standing around waiting to make a save. So when the ball flew 50 yards behind the goal there was only one person who had to go and get it. After all, the outfield players could do with a rest and the keeper could do with some exercise. When a game was in its third hour the opportunity of a breather, as the goalie retrieved the ball, was welcomed by both sides. Often players would sit down and have a chat or sunbathe. Sometimes, getting the ball back would take an age, as it ended up stuck under a car, in a tree, or in a patch of nettles or other such ferocious shrubs.

Occasionally the goalie would take the opportunity offered by this lapse in concentration to launch an ambitious counter-strike. A slow, meandering walk back to his goal area would become a pounding gallop just as the goalie reached the pitch. Bodies, previously slumped, lifeless, on the playing field would burst into response with shouts of disgust at such an underhand tactic.

Usually the keeper would get as far down the pitch as possible then hit a long-shot just before the opposition goalie could get back into nets. The hasty attack did not always result in a goal, but it regularly added to the excitement and prompted heated discussions about the legality of the keeper's actions.

How does this nostalgic ramble relate to modern football? Well, as we all know the goalkeeper plays under a different set of rules to the rest of the players. They are up there with pandas and tigers on the WWF's list of protected species. We want to introduce the 'goalie's golden rule' back into the game. No more ball boys to do the keeper's dirty work. When the ball goes behind, it is up to the goalie

to get it back. Hard luck if there are opposition fans behind the goal. It's down to the goalkeepers. If they protest,
the referee must recite the mantra, 'goalie's golden rule...
always get the bloody ball' before theatrically issuing an
automatic red card.

Imagine Van der Sar climbing into the Kop to wrestle
the ball back from the fans in the last minutes of a match?
Everyone talks about reconnecting the players with the fans.
Well, this is their chance. In some small way it would help
to counterbalance the rules that protect the goalkeeper. It
would also give them some much-needed physical exertion.
They might even think twice about dramatically tipping the
ball over the bar instead of bloody well catching it.

Gordon Ramsay's F-word

The F-word in question isn't the usual foul-mouthed exple-
tive – it's football.

Celebrities who play on their football credentials really
get our goat, and, in this instance that goat would be seared,
then slow-cooked in an Aga, garnished with rosemary,
served with sauté potatoes and washed down with a shot of
crème de menthe. Possibly.

Yes, we are talking about Gordon effin' Ramsay. We've
ranted and raved about nouveaux fans who – despite thinking that football was invented in 1992 – use their supposed
'celebrity' to wangle slots on television and radio talking
about football. Gordon doesn't quite fall into that category,
but he has been a bit of a tinker when it comes to his footballing past.

Ramsay is famous for two things: swearing and cooking.
He's a cook, who swears – a lot. Nothing particularly amazing
about that you'd think? We all swear like troopers when we
forget about the pizza we'd popped in the oven and end up
having to crunch our way through its charred remains. But
Gordon cooks and swears *on the telly*. His shows are massive
ratings hits.

The other thing we all know about Gordon Ramsay is
this: he used to be a professional footballer – with Glasgow
Rangers. Being a footballer made his transformation
to celebrity cook all the more amazing, and it was also
frequently wheeled out to explain and/or excuse his
swearing. The football thing was a hook to set him apart
from that other famous cooking chap, Jamie Oliver. While
Jamie bobbed and weaved around East End markets on his
scooter acting all chipper, Gordon was the tough guy who'd
played for Rangers and swore at his staff.

This is where the problems began. Gordon is about five
years older than us, which means he was probably playing

for Rangers when we were at the height of our statistical prowess – around about 1984. Thing is, we don't remember him. Now, we don't profess to remember every promising youngster to play for the Old Firm, but we thought it strange that it didn't ring any bells. Especially as he sounded like a curious amalgam of Gordon Stewart from *Roy of the Rovers* and Sir Alf Ramsey (himself fresh from a short spell managing Melchester Rovers, as Roy lay in a coma in hospital in the self-same comic). But Gordon was adamant. On *Desert Island Discs* in 2002 he claimed he was a part of the first team squad and had played three matches. In his autobiography, he had downgraded slightly, saying he'd played for the first team twice, 'but only in friendlies or pre-season'. With Ramsay's 'career' being cut short through injury at the age of 18, you'd think he'd be a little less vague about such high-points – and able to remember stuff like: the opposition, the location, the scores?

Ramsay also claims that the great Jock Wallace and his assistant Archie Knox personally called time on his playing days by summoning him into their office to deliver the bad news. This version of events was disputed by Knox, who claimed he first set eyes on Ramsay in 1996 when he launched his first cook book.

The *Daily Mail* seemingly confirmed our vague suspicions in an article in March 2009 entitled, 'How Gordon Ramsay lied about his football career to raise his celebrity profile.' The paper quoted Glasgow Rangers historian Robert McElroy saying, 'Ramsay never played for the Rangers first team, either in friendlies or pre-season.'

It seems Gordon Ramsay was a triallist who, as a schoolboy, travelled up to Glasgow in the holidays as part of the club's youth policy. Then, just 18 years old, he hurt his knee and set about becoming a famous cook.

So, why would Gordon look to embellish his football career? Let's face it, if he'd caught the eye of Rangers scouts, he was probably a bit tasty. We'll probably never know, but the football back story certainly seemed to suit his television persona: footballers swear, and Ramsay wasn't averse to dishing out the Alex Ferguson 'hairdryer' treatment when confronted with underperforming staff, especially if it made great television.

It certainly shows how far football's popularity stretches, if claiming to be an ex-professional boosts your media career. We just think it's a bit sad. We've always been shit at football and proud of it and we've never felt the need to say we turned out for Stockport County. So, Gordon, we'd like to offer you the chance to prove how good you are – play us at five-a-side. We know you took part in ITV's *Soccer Aid*, but your early substitution only set more alarm bells ringing in our heads. As genuine football nuts, given a once in a lifetime opportunity to play at a packed Old Trafford, we wouldn't limp off injured. Injuries are for wimps, not tough-tackling, tough-talking celebrity cooks.

So here's your chance: sign up to our Famous Five (see Famous five-a-side) and give us a tonking at football. We can handle the swearing, but can you handle the post-match *Nightmares?*

Here's to you Michael Robinson...

Michael Robinson was one of many strikers bought to re-place Kenny Dalglish at Anfield in the mid 1980s. He lasted one season, scored six goals and won the European Cup as a playing substitute. He was also a Republic of Ireland interna-tional. His last move saw him arrive at Osasuna in Spain. And what happened next shocked a nation (or three).

Unlike many of the players who went abroad in the 1980s, Robinson learnt to speak the language of his new country – fluently. This may seem obvious if you want to make a success of working abroad, but most footballers don't bother. And, after scoring 87 goals in 352 appearances he decided to stay in Spain. This wasn't because he wanted to open a bar when he finished playing – he left that to the Linekers.

No, Michael Robinson became a football pundit. First on the radio station Cadena SER's *El Larguero* and then on Canal+ where he hosted *El día después* for 14 years. This was a major surprise to everyone. Michael was never regarded as a superstar, and many were shocked to see a journeyman footballer do so well as a pundit overseas. Would the British public have accepted an unknown foreign footballer's opinions? We doubt it; the poor soul would've been hounded out of the country by an irate mob of *Daily Mail* readers, demanding jobs for our ex-pros.

These days, there are a plethora of overseas players who have invaded punditry, coaching and management and the British public have accepted them. But Michael Robinson broke new ground.

We salute you, Michael Robinson, for becoming a suc-cess in Spain. Thanks to your incisive tactical comments they won the European Championship. Cheers, really helpful.

Hero for a day

Some players are lucky enough to be remembered for something that pricked a nation's conscience. And for some that one moment comes to define their career. It may be a cup final appearance, an international hat-trick or it may be jumping feet first into the crowd to kung-fu kick a fan. Sometimes these moments are a blessing, but more often than not they are a curse – and there's nothing worse than being remembered for being really good in a schoolboy international.

For many, the end of the football season in the 1970s and early '80s meant one thing: live matches on TV, principally the FA and European Cup finals and international matches, but the BBC and ITV were always looking to fill a Saturday afternoon with a football match. Especially games they could pick up for peanuts – schoolboy internationals fitted the bill perfectly.

At first glance, a schoolboy international may not sound that interesting. Only die-hard fans would know any of the participants. Commentators would struggle gamely to identify each player, often mentioning the club they played for every time they touched the ball. Yet, due to the scarcity of live football on the box, these games had a loyal TV following. These schoolboy fixtures were played at Wembley on a Saturday afternoon at the end of May or the beginning of June, and always in high temperatures. There is one particular schoolboy match that stands out above all others and that was England v Scotland in 1980.

A run-of-the-mill Saturday afternoon for us was brightened up by this game. It might have only been a junior fixture, but it turned into a classic tussle between old foes. The game had been 'pure Roy of the Rovers stuff' and, as usual, it ended in tragedy for England. The game finished 5-4 to Scotland, but a young lad called Paul Rideout scored a hat-trick for England. Rideout was the name on everyone's lips at school the following Monday morning. As the goals flew in, the commentator duly reminded us that Paul Rideout had a great future ahead of him. Oh yes, and did we mention he was only 15, because the pundits definitely did? The big pitch, heat and the age of the participants combined to allow gaps all over the pitch – gaps that Paul Rideout exploited. The game was stretched almost from the start. You could tell it was desperate stuff, because everyone had their socks rolled down, even the referee. The match was watched by millions and gave Rideout instant celebrity.

Everyone knew Paul Rideout, but his game never quite reached the same heights again. His playing career spanned 22 years; he played for England U21s; made more than 570 appearances for various clubs including Aston Villa, AS Bari, Southampton and Rangers; he scored 151 goals, including the winner in the 1995 FA Cup final for Everton against Manchester United, but he never quite eclipsed that hat-trick for England schoolboys. That afternoon at Wembley became a millstone around his neck. A television audience of millions would only ever remember the 15-year-old Rideout scoring three goals for England and still ending up on the losing side. It was a classic tale of too much, too young – a schoolboy error, if you like. See also Rod Thomas.

Hitman and Him, The

Nightmare-inducing fuzzy screens and the endless spooling of Teletext pages disappeared in the early 1980s, as ITV entered the brave new world of through-the-night telly. Football fans everywhere were in for a treat. One evening we were scanning the schedules for programmes with either a hint of erotica or tenuous football content, when we stumbled across a show that offered both at once – we had found *Best & Marsh*. It was on at 2.55am. Luckily, our clunky Betamax recorder had a primitive timer knob, so we could watch it the next day. Boy, we were in for a treat.

Best & Marsh rivalled anything Pete Waterman and Michaela Strachan could throw at us. Like an X-rated version of *Saint & Greavsie*, these two mavericks reminisced at length about their playing days. It was cheap TV and it showed, but for football aficionados it harked back to a golden era of the game, full of characters and brought to life by the chuckling presenters. It was a vehicle for two popular ex-players to chat and make a couple of quid. Of course, the match footage saved the show; no matter what hour of the day it was always a pleasure to watch George Best and Rodney Marsh in their '70s pomp.

Despite saturation coverage, it is hard to believe we will see such a show again. Ex-footballers invariably act as pundits, or occasionally graduate to the role of sub-standard anchormen. And, sadly, the game is bereft of characters like Best and Marsh. Would we really be interested in the world according to *Lampard & Gerrard*? Sure, they are great players, but they have little ability to engage with the fan. Their football does the talking. And they don't need the money either. It is a lot harder to be a loveable rascal in the professional, money-orientated game of today.

There is hope. Perhaps *Dave* will listen to our plea to re-run *Best & Marsh* in its original graveyard slot. It could go back-to-back with *The Hitman and Her*.

Horn of Africa, the

What is it with FIFA and fun? Perhaps the most enjoyable thing about the 2009 Confederations Cup in South Africa was the vuvuzela.

No, 'vuvuzela' isn't some local liquor quaffed by FIFA dignitaries in the plush air-conditioned hotels of Jo'burg. Nor is it some dangerous tropical disease. A vuvuzela is the noisy plastic trumpet blown by fans. It creates a continuous, low buzzing noise that sounds like a cross between a burglar alarm going off in the distance and a swarm of particularly agitated mosquitos. And, for some reason, FIFA was considering banning them.

Apparently, broadcasters complained that the humming sound was confusing audiences and drowning out commentary – if you were listening to Jonathan Pearce continue to struggle with the transition from radio to television on BBC3 during the Confederations Cup, then you were probably quite grateful.

But it wasn't just broadcasters. Spain's midfielder Xabi Alonso was livid. He said: 'I think they should be banned. They make it very difficult for the players to communicate with each other and to concentrate.' Maybe the low humming noise was interfering with his finely-tuned, long-distance passing radar – he certainly didn't try one of his trademark goals from inside his own half, for which we can only blame the vuvuzela.

To his credit, Sepp Blatter was feeling horny (sorry, worrying mental image alert): 'It's a local sound and I don't know how it is possible to stop it,' he said. 'It's noisy, it's energy, rhythm, music, dance, drums.' This latter part of Sepp's quote took the mental image to a terrifying new level: Sepp with the horn, rhythmically gyrating to the Real Sounds of Africa.

Hopefully, FIFA will see sense and not kowtow to the demands of over-sensitive broadcasters. For us, it was only the constant buzz from a thousand plastic trumpets that kept us awake during the Confederations Cup. With any luck, the vuvuzela will be allowed to accompany us for the duration of the World Cup.

As Sepp said: 'This is Africa. We have to adapt a little.'

Hot-Shot Hamish v The Cannonball Kid v Murdo McLeod

Hot-Shot Hamish v The Cannonball Kid. What a battle this was: forget your top strikers of the 1970s and '80s, no-one could compare with these two hard-hitters. Both famed for their explosive shooting, they made Racey's Rocket look like a girly back pass.

Hamish Balfour was a Hebridean behemoth, and owner of the hardest shot in soccer. He started life in *Scorcher*, before moving to *Roy of the Rovers* via *Tiger*. A giant of a man – who wore his shirt several sizes too small to emphasise the point – he played for Princes Park in the Scottish to division under svengali boss Ian McWhacker. Hamish showed little regard for anything that stood in his way. His party piece was to literally burst the net. How much did that cost the Scottish Premier League each season? Goalkeepers were knocked into the back of the net with frightening regularity, but injuries were few, and there was little concern for their well-being. Hamish's shot was immense and, much like Rory Delap's trademark long throw, no one quite knew how to deal with it.

There were two things from the comic strip that were hard to understand. First, if you were McWhacker, surely you would have Hamish taking goal-kicks and free-kicks from all over the pitch, launching the ball at pace into the area, or just going for goal. Sure, accuracy is important, but with the hardest shot in football it would be tempting to use it at every opportunity.

Secondly, why didn't a 'big' club swoop to sign him? There must've been hundreds of clubs desperate for a bit of Hamish's fire power? Maybe he couldn't travel with his pet sheep, McMutton, because of the quarantine laws? Or perhaps a new club would have insisted he wore proper fitting shirts?

In later years, Hamish teamed-up with Mighty Mouse – an overweight, spectacle-wearing, part-time footballer from the English First Division, who signed for Princes Park after a brief holiday in Scotland. The pair formed an unlikely partnership, but somehow it worked. Eventually the dynamic duo transferred to Glengow Rangers where they were reunited with manager McWhacker. Hamish might've played his entire career in Scotland, but his legend was known the world over – Hot-Shot Hamish and Mighty Mouse's story was translated into various languages. In Sweden Hamish was simply 'Super-Mac' (we're surprised Malcolm Macdonald didn't sue) while in France, 'Hamish and Mouse' became the delightful 'Hamish La Foudre and Mousie L'Eclair'.

Despite this global notoriety, there was a rival for Hot-Shot Hamish's crown. Enter 'The Cannonball Kid', a cartoon strip with a more realistic feel that was found in *Scoop*. If you are searching for an analogy, The Cannonball Kid was the gritty realism of *Starsky and Hutch* to Hot-Shot Hamish's *Dukes of Hazzard* crazy comedy antics – sort of.

'The Cannonball Kid' was actually Jimmy Weston, a young lad who studied piano at the local music college in Baypool. He was spotted at a fair where his shooting prowess in a 'Beat the Goalie' sideshow persuaded a scout to invite him down for a trial at Baypool. Now, here's the twist – Jimmy knew absolutely nothing about football. Who would have thought it? His Aunt insisted he continued his musical education, so after helping Baypool win promotion he went on a world tour with the Grand Symphony Orchestra. This must have been where the *High School Musical* writers got their ideas – clearly Troy Bolton wasn't the first jock to have talents in other areas.

Jimmy wrestled with this dilemma throughout the life of the comic strip. However, 'The Cannonball Kid' did not run continuously in *Scoop*. It was a returning feature that amounted to three separate stories. The second story involved him playing in the band 'The Rock Revival' and having to gain the approval of his manager at Baypool so that he could go on tour (after he'd initially disguised his identity in the band). To make the tour he had to win the League Cup – which, of course, he duly did.

In our favourite story, he signed for Saskabay Tigers in North America. Here he met unscrupulous club owner JJ Canmire, who even tried to send a look-alike back to Baypool! It was during this series that we learnt that there were no draws in the North American Soccer League.

'The Cannonball Kid' was more realistic than Hamish (though only just) and had a little more depth to the storylines. Shaun was particularly interested as he played euphonium in a local brass band and this often clashed with his football commitments – as a result he always had a soft spot for Jimmy.

Hamish Balfour and Jimmy Weston were two great players linked by the power of their shot. Sadly, they never came up against each other. Each story made us think about football in a different way and it is sad that kids today no longer learn about football and life through comics.

In the real world, there is one footballer whom everyone remembers for having a hard shot – Branco. Older readers may envisage him as the cunning inmate friend of Fletch in *Porridge*. We are sorry to inform you that his name was Blanco. We're talking about Branco, the Brazilian left back.

In the 1990 World Cup, Murdo McLeod, a flaxen-haired Scot in the great tradition of Hot-Shot Hamish, was minding his own business when he was hit in the head by an Exocet from Branco. Gary McAllister alleges that following the shot Murdo did not know which way he was kicking and was duly substituted. Some would claim, based on their performances, that Scotland *never* knew which way they were kicking in World Cup Finals, but we prefer to say they've just been unlucky.

Most footballers, amateur and professional, have had a ball struck into their face, but few have been substituted.

Apart from the endless TV replays of McLeod's misfortune, we don't remember much else about Scotland at Italia '90 and neither does Murdo. Really, he should be eternally grateful he wasn't struck by a shot from Hot-Shot Hamish or The Cannonball Kid – that would've really smarted.

I say UEFA, you say UEFA

George and Ira Gershwin nailed it when they sang: 'Ueeefa, uayefa, tomato, tomahto! Let's call the Champions League off.' And that was in 1937.

You'd have thought this would've been the first thing Platini got his teeth into after becoming president. Does he even know which organisation he is working for – Ueeefa or Uayefa?

Sod trying to redress the balance of power in modern football. Sod trying to award Champions League places fairly. Sort out the bloody pronunciation.

While we are on the subject, we are convinced that when the UEFA Cup replaced the Inter-City Fairs in 1971 it was referred to as the EUFA Cup. Who are EUFA? Splitters, like the Judean Popular People's Front?

If the cap fits

They've brought back the bloke who walks out in front of the teams at Wembley holding the FA Cup (last seen in about 1974), so now it is time for the FA to do something about international caps.

There's no point in going through the expensive process of manufacturing international caps if players are not going to wear them. The England team currently sport an impressively old-school kit (in an Eton or Harrow kind of way), so perhaps the time is right for them to wear their caps as well.

It would look dead smart and it could be rolled out to other countries. National headdress could become a required feature of international football. It would certainly make the early stages of World Cup qualifying a darn sight more exciting. Headgear coming adrift during a match would result in a mandatory yellow card. Lose your hat twice in a game and there'd be a compulsory caning in the headmaster's study.

So, there you go, that's our entirely practical solution to the problem of international caps. No, really, you're welcome.

Instant replay

Remember when FA Cup ties seemed to last for ever? Replay after replay stretching into eternity and creating a fixture pile-up that would only begin to unravel in early May.

Multiple replays were part of FA Cup folklore. Fulham needed twelve matches to reach the 1975 cup final. They edged past Hull City 1-0 in the third round after a second replay, and required four matches (the original tie plus three replays) before finally overcoming Nottingham Forest 2-1 at the City Ground in round four.

Even their semi-final against Birmingham City required a replay, and then was only won after extra-time. For Fulham the marathon ultimately ended in disappointment, going down to West Ham and two Alan Taylor goals in the final at Wembley.

In 1979, it took eventual winners Arsenal four replays to get past Sheffield Wednesday in the third round of the competition. The five fixtures took place in the space of sixteen days between the 6th and 22nd of January. And, Arsène, you complain of fixture congestion?

The fact that the replays took place a matter of days after the original fixture was of vital importance and, ultimately, proved to be the undoing of never-ending matches. Tune into the reading of the classified football results on *Sports Report* on FA Cup day during the 1970s and '80s and the result of drawn games would be followed by James Alexander Gordon uttering the immortal words, 'Replay on Tuesday'. In an instant, details of the fixture were relayed to all and sundry; all the players, officials and supporters had to do was turn up.

Unfortunately, this sort of spontaneity has no place in a health and safety obsessed world. And a couple of days' notice is no longer enough for the local police force to juggle their commitments and re-arrange shifts. Heaven forbid a handful of traffic cops being taken off duty to police a football match.

So, in the 1991/92 season a ludicrous ten-day rule was enforced. Gone were the instant replays and in came a ten-day lag between the original tie and the replayed game. The havoc this was going to cause prompted FA suits to rise from their slumber and act. Multiple replays were outlawed, and extra-time and penalties were introduced at the end of the first replayed game. Semi-finals and finals didn't get replays at all. Of far too much significance, they were reduced to the lottery of penalties.

In a stroke, the romance of the cup was dealt another almighty blow. No more FA Cup Odysseys of Homeric proportions; instead sudden-death shoot-outs for the 'I want it now' generation.

Izzy Clarke

Is Izzy Clarke the new Penny Race? We spent much of the 1980s dreaming about Penny Race, and now we do the same with Izzy Clarke. The fact that Izzy is a real person and not a pencil sketch can be considered progress of sorts (that's our counsellor's take on it, anyway).

It started innocently enough, being gently soothed by her voice on 5 Live. Then, they went and introduced *606* interactive. Now, every Tuesday we get to *watch* Ms Clarke act as the foil for Danny Baker's bonkers creativity. Her football knowledge is impeccable, and she even had the common decency to humour the humourless Tim Lovejoy on the Wednesday night version of the show.

You can keep your Sky Sports dollybirds. Give us an hour with Izzy any day – and not in a dirty way, either. We'd absolutely love to co-present the occasional episode of *606*. Living in a fantasy world? You bet.

Joy of Six, the

Here's a thing: we are both obsessed by France's 1982 World Cup squad. In our heads the '82 final wasn't Italy v Germany, it was France v Brazil – two of the most beautiful teams in football history.

We love the French side. We love their iconic Adidas shirts (and despair of the many shoddy replicas that keep appearing on eBay. The devil's in the detail – the collar was white but the V-neck was blue – you goons!). We love Platini, Giresse and Tigana. And we still wince every time someone mentions Patrick Battiston. But most of all we love Didier Six.

Didier had hair like a mop-topped Beatle, only wilder. He had a swagger, his socks were rolled down and he looked like he had just fallen out of bed. He was the glue that bound the 1982 squad together. Despite this, we can't help thinking that manager Michel Hidalgo missed a trick: he gave Didier Six the No.19 shirt. Surely, he could've worn six? Christian Lopez of St Etienne, who wore the No.6 shirt, started only the match against England, so he was hardly a mainstay of the side. Six deserved that shirt. Imagine the fun Barry Davies *et al* would've had if Six had been wearing six. Then imagine the branding opportunities: the *Six* clothing range, the aftershave. We can't sleep at night for thinking about it.

Don't even get us started about Sep(t) Blatter...

Kettering to Palestine

Shirt sponsorship has been on a bit of a road trip: from Kettering to Palestine to be precise. Let's hope they fitted a new set of tyres before setting off on the long journey from Rockingham Road to Ramallah.

The unsightly flocking on the front of football shirts used to be a tribute to capitalism: if you were Premier League, you'd probably be part of some global branding push involving a mobile phone, an airline or an online betting emporium; further down the pyramid, you could be advertising anything from the local kebab house to the undertakers. We've got no proof, but we'd like to think it was Chupa Chups' sponsorship of Sheffield Wednesday that prompted Naomi Klein to pen *No Logo*, her seminal 446-page rant against consumerism. But, things are changing. Since we last wrote there's been a seismic shift in the world of shirt sponsorship.

Barcelona led the way, agreeing a deal with UNICEF, but we never thought it would catch on. After all, Barca are different – before UNICEF their shirts had remained proudly sponsorship free. Now, a number of other teams are following Barcelona's lead and ditching their corporate sponsors in favour of promoting charitable organisations. Aston Villa carry the logo of West Midlands-based charity, Acorns Children's Hospice on their shirts. To celebrate their 125th year, Leicester City left their home shirt sponsor-free, but have handed over the space on their away shirt to local hospice charity, LOROS.

In September 2008, after the sudden collapse of holiday company XL, West Ham United were left sponsorless and were forced to play several matches with embarrassing iron-on number patches obscuring the defunct sponsors' logo. However, their new deal with online betting company SBO-BET also ensured increased publicity for the Bobby Moore

Fund for Cancer Research UK – the deal stipulated that all West Ham's academy and junior sides wore shirts bearing the charity's logo, and that all junior replica kits sold also carried the Bobby Moore insignia.

This recent benevolence on the part of our football clubs is both welcome and surprising – it's a development nobody would've predicted prior to Barcelona's agreement with UNICEF. We hope in our hearts that this altruism is everything to do with the realisation of a football club's position in the community and its ability to help others and absolutely nothing to do with the global economic downturn. We'd hate to think that clubs are just filling dead space caused by the credit crunch.

We said at the start that shirt sponsorship in football has been on something of a road trip, and that trip began and ended at Rockingham Road, Kettering. It is well documented that non-league Kettering Town were the first football club in England to embrace shirt sponsorship – Derek Dougan's men running out in shirts emblazoned with the legend 'Kettering Tyres' way back in January 1976. Almost 33 years to the day, The Poppies were at it again.

On Saturday 3rd January 2009, Kettering players took to the pitch – in a televised FA Cup tie against Eastwood Town – wearing shirts 'sponsored' by Palestine Aid. Kettering Town chairman, Imraan Ladak had given the space on the shirts to Interpal, a charity which distributes aid in the Palestinian territories. Ladack had no personal links to Palestine, but had been moved to act after witnessing the scenes of destruction that had resulted from an escalation of hostilities in Gaza in the weeks preceding the match.

Obviously, Palestine is a particularly unusual issue for a football club to broach, especially through shirt sponsorship – the politics surrounding the region never fails to ignite debate – but for Ladack and Kettering the motives weren't political but humanitarian. In an interview with *The Guardian*, he said, 'I just think there are certain areas in the world that are in desperate need of humanitarian assistance, for whatever reason and Palestine is the one that's suffering the most.'

It was a bold move by Kettering Town, and one that brings a certain symmetry to the world of shirt sponsorship. Kettering were at the vanguard of commercial sponsorship in football and it is fitting that they should also be one of the clubs leading the way in donating shirt space to charitable causes.

So, where does shirt sponsorship go from here? We don't expect every club to drop their lucrative commercial agreements, but it is always nice to see a club giving something back to the community, be it a local hospice like Acorns or a global charitable organisation like UNICEF. And, short of our Premiership stars deciding collectively to donate their mega-bucks salaries to charity and play for the love of the game, giving over shirt advertising to worthy causes seems like a fantastic way to show that football hasn't – as many of us have long suspected – disappeared up its own arse.

Kitsch clash

Previous generations of nostalgia junkies had to rely on hazy memories, exaggerated anecdotes or musty old football magazines when summoning the ghosts of football past – we just type a few choice words into Google.

The internet has revolutionised the past. You can watch the past on YouTube; you can research the past on Wikipedia; and you can buy up large swathes of the past on eBay. The worldwide web has made the rich tapestry of football heritage available to us all for the price of a broadband connection.

Pouring over statistics or settling pub squabbles is great, but the internet really comes into its own when you start looking for old football shirts. Being Thatcher's children, we grew up in the shadow of both irreversible industrial decline *and* Coventry City's brown away kit. Evidence of Maggie's wholesale destruction was all around us: first she took our milk, then as PM she set about taking everything else. And, by 1982, it was impossible to validate the existence of Cov's controversial brown kit. No one could lay their hands on proof of its existence. It was the talk of the playground – an urban myth for the Panini generation. In school, the dispute always went like this: 'My Dad says Coventry City used to play in a brown kit,' 'Duuuuuuuuur, no one plays in BROWN, you slaphead!' There then followed a minor scuffle as the disbelieving kid tried unsuccessfully to slap the head of the other lad.

Of course, thanks to the internet, we now know that Coventry City did indeed sport a chocolate brown away kit between 1978 and 1980. It was made by Admiral and had iconic parallel stripes on the front that continued onto the shorts. But as kids, the kit remained a myth. We scoured back issues of *Shoot!* and *Roy of the Rovers*, but the best we could find was a grainy photo of Bobby McDonald rolling about in the mud. Of course, the photo was in black and white and so didn't help at all. By the time we reached university in the early 1990s Coventry City's brown away kit had assumed legendary status; widely acknowledged as The Holy Grail of football kitsch. Despite this, Nick's tutor couldn't have been more condescending when Nick suggested that he wrote his final year dissertation* on the cultural significance of Coventry's chocolate brown kit – Nick had planned 10,000 words describing how the seemingly random choice of a brown kit was in fact a subconscious representation of the industrial decay that gripped the Midlands during the late 1970s and early '80s.

Now, Cov's kit can be Googled in seconds, and before you know what's happened your eyes are assaulted by the mind-bending combination of that chocolate brown strip and Ian Wallace's outrageous ginger afro. And that's it, mystery solved. Coventry's kit *did* exist. But that's not the end, oh no. The internet has allowed us to widen our search for football's most kitsch kit.

As fast as we can recall bonkers kits from seasons past, the internet validates their existence. Didn't Notts County wear some kind of tartan monstrosity as an away kit in the early '90s? Yep, 'twas 1994/95 and it looked ludicrous. And didn't Celtic have a mint green away kit with a graph graphic across the front, that looked like a visual representation of the boom/bust economy of the 1980s? Yep, 1991/92, made by Umbro. What about the rash of garish acid house kits worn by everyone from Bristol Rovers to Stockport County in the early 1990s? All present and correct. And all this without mentioning Hull City's tiger print or Athletic Bilbao's surreal tomato ketchup blobs.

There are so many dodgy kits out there that – if we didn't have jobs, or families to feed – we could easily lose ourselves for days in an online world of tacky polyester. At least we thought we could. Then we stumbled across the most kitsch kit of all-time. A kit that *is* The Holy Grail.

The kit we refer to was worn by Caribous of Colorado, a team who played just a solitary season in the North American Soccer League in 1978. The Caribous played in the exquisitely named Mile High Stadium in Denver, Colorado. They hold the record for the worst season in NASL history, winning eight games, losing 22 and, in the process, amassing an unfathomable 81 points – we can only assume they picked up most of those points in the dressage, but more of that in a moment.

The history of the Caribous may have been short and sweet, but their playing roster contained a couple of intriguing names: there was Brian Budd, the Canadian, better known for winning *World Superstars* three years running from 1978 to 1980 (demolishing the seemingly invincible British entrant Brian Jacks in the process); then there was Brian Tinnion**, the former Wrexham stalwart who swapped the rigours of the football league for the glamour of the NASL, spending a season with both the New York Cosmos and Team Hawaii before decamping to Colorado.

But the Caribous of Colorado won't be remembered for any of this. The Caribous will only ever be remembered for their kit. It is almost impossible to describe; we'll have a go, but we strongly recommend that you Google it, pronto. There were two versions of the kit, the 'home' kit and the 'road' version. The colours were slightly different but the design remained the same. The kit featured the obligatory monster collars (this was the late '70s after all) and also a ridiculous oversized Caribous logo on the chest, but the shirt's distinguishing feature was its suede tassels. Yes, that's right – TASSELS. They were astonishing, running across the front of the chest and all around the back. Think Davy Crockett meets Dolly Parton meets Vegas-era Elvis. A country and western horror show in tan and white.

By the time you added a name and number on the back (above the tassels, obviously) and number on the front and on both sleeves, you had the most kitsch kit of all time.

A thousand words couldn't begin to paint this cowboy/ soccer nightmare. So we are going to stop right here. All we can say is check it out on the internet: you won't be disappointed. Meanwhile, we are going to sit tight and wait for some trendy young kit designer at Nike or Adidas to stumble across the same photo and instigate a tasselled suede rival. Chelsea running out in blue suede tassels? Don't laugh, it will probably happen.

* It's called social history, mate (and look at me now, writing books about it – that's showed you, eh?).
** Not to be confused with the other Brian Tinnion of Bristol City fame.

Language, Timothy

Language at football has always been 'choice', 'industrial' or just plain 'obscene'. Swearing at football hasn't got any better or worse down the years: it's actually one of the game's few constants – a foul-mouthed volley of abuse that links the workers stumbling out of the factory and into the ground on a Saturday in the 1930s to the overpaid Premiership primadonnas of the 21st century. Fans and players have always sworn like troopers and always will – irrespective of any FA campaigns or directives. You don't need to be a lip-reader to get the gist of the average on-pitch exchange, and the slo-motion replays on *Match of the Day* only confirm what we already knew.

Going to football as a kid was like jumping headfirst into *Roger's Profanisaurus*. We heard words on the terraces that we knew we could never repeat over Sunday lunch; although if we were feeling brave we'd sometimes give them an airing in a playground slanging-match. It was an education, an education that largely consisted of beery blokes screaming swear words at the tops of their voices – usually in the general direction of the referee. Even more awe-inspiring to your average eleven-year-old was the communal swear-a-longs, that seemed to involve the entire crowd bawling such delicacies as 'Who's the wanker in the black?' and 'He's here, he's there, he's every f*****g-where, Sammy Lee!'

Of course, we look back now and wince. All that swearing seems both unnecessary and crass. We ask ourselves what will happen when we start taking our own kids to football on a regular basis? Will we adopt our dads' take on events and just completely ignore the profanity that's exploding all around us?

The only thing worse than indoctrinating your children into a life of communal swearing is taking a genteel friend or relative to a football match. Going to non-league football only exacerbates the problem, as you can literally hear every word uttered on the pitch. Nick suffered personal trauma of this kind when he took his father-in-law to a local game: after fluffing an easy chance, the centre-forward of the team we were supporting managed to construct a highly complex sentence entirely out of swear words – really loud, about four feet from where we were standing. True to form, Nick tried to pretend it had never happened.

Swearing is a constant, but the language of football is constantly evolving. Our occasional attendance at non-league grounds around the country has alerted us to this phenomenon: football's language is being systematically reduced to a string of one-word utterances. Gone are the days of managers barking complex instructions to players from the sidelines. Instead, tactical and motivational encouragement is now issued with maximum efficiency and minimum effort.

You think we're bonkers? Get down to your local ground and see for yourself. Here's a random selection: shuffle; settle; relax; finish; tighter; release; deliver; carry; time; hold. And that's just for starters. It's the English language distilled to its purest form. We can only assume this non-league future-speak continues after the game: beer; döner; shag?

Inevitably, the swearing and these new one-word utterances frequently collide and make beautiful music, like: 'f*****g deliver,' 'f*****g settle,' 'f*****g' pretty much anything. Classy, eh? The words might be fewer but really nothing has changed at all – and we're not sure whether to be depressed or comforted.

Lofty peaks and dizzy rascals

It's not what you think. British grime sensation Dizzee Rascal hasn't ditched Armand Van Helden in favour of '70s Melchester Rovers centre-half, Lofty Peak, for a bonkers remix of his 'Bonkers' single (and if you didn't understand any of that last sentence, don't worry, neither did we).

No, on flicking through Tim Hill's *A Photographic History of English Football*, we were struck by a phenomenon strangely absent from the modern game. It's something we can remember going on at matches when we were kids, but it more or less disappeared overnight with the advent of modern, out-of-town, all-seater stadia.

We are referring to the dangerous vantage points spectators would assume in order to watch a big match. In our youth, floodlight pylons were fair game for fans who wished to eschew the packed terrace for a better view and a loftier perch. Sitting awkwardly on the pylons was a risky business that usually involved traversing some badly erected barbed-wire defences, but once in place, the lower reaches of the pylon offered fantastic views and the opportunity to piss on your fellow fans from a reasonable height. The only problem with this particular vantage point was you still had to pay to get in.

More resourceful fans would look to secure a perch outside the ground. This often involved local scallywags climbing trees. A photograph from the 1914 Cup final at Crystal Palace shows hundreds of non-paying customers standing on the embankment above the ground (which was situated in a natural bowl), but many more fans had taken to nesting in the trees, like woodbine-smoking rooks. Or maybe we were mistaken: they weren't there for the football at all; they were looking for Osprey eggs and taking part in the other popular sport of the early 20th century – stealing birds' eggs.

These days, you rarely see a bloke up a tree, whether poaching eggs or watching the football – and we blame satellite TV. Why venture out, when you can crack open a beer and sit in front of the telly? Occasionally, you'll see fans watching a game from the balcony of a nearby block of flats – it's not quite in the same league as sitting in the canopy of a birch tree for 90 minutes, but it is dedication of sorts, especially if the flats only offer a partial view of the pitch.

The other great 'lost' vantage point at football – and, perhaps, the most dangerous – is the view from the roof of the stand. Once again our memory was jogged by a photograph: a shot of a packed Stamford Bridge (stop sniggering) in 1945, during the visit of Dynamo Moscow, shows the gabled roof packed with fans – including one chap casually propped up against a weathervane. Today's health and safety crew would be having forty-fits, and we have to say it looked pretty precarious – but again it highlighted the dedication and determination of fans to watch the match. Of course, there's a certain irony to a photograph showing Stamford Bridge packed – literally – to the rafters for a meaningless European tie (the Russian team were touring Britain in an era before competitive European football) when these days they often struggle to fill the ground in the early stages of the Champions League.

These old photographs confirm how times have changed. Before football was a 24/7 televisual commodity, fans would do anything to catch the game. Being at the match was all that mattered, and if you couldn't afford a ticket or the game was a sell-out, then you'd risk life and limb to secure a decent perch.

It's a shame those days have gone. There was nothing we liked more than waiting to see which of the dizzy rascals in bell-bottomed flares wedged precariously between two floodlight girders would come a cropper first – it was usually a darn sight more exciting than the football.

Lovejoy division

For several years, we've had reason to believe that Tim Lovejoy is the most despised man in football – the personal embodiment of all that is wrong with the beautiful game. Now we are not so sure.

But, before we cast judgement, let's rewind to the very beginning – a time before the first ball had been kicked and the first satellite dish installed in anger. Yes, it's 1992, and Lovejoy (plus a handful of celebrity mates) finds himself stumbling out of an exclusive brasserie in Notting Hill, absent-mindedly kicking an empty Coke can into the gutter. 'Hey, great kick Timbo,' shouts a good-looking, posh bloke in a home counties accent. 'Yeah, pretty cool wasn't it, Rufus?' Tim guffaws.

The next day Lovejoy took his discovery to a commissioning editor at Sky TV and, thus, the global phenomenon of football was born.

Lovejoy could have sat back on his laurels and coined in the royalties from his invention, but he didn't. In 1996, he teamed up with Helen Chamberlain to host *Soccer AM*, a Saturday morning television show that borrowed heavily from Timmy Mallett's seminal *Wacaday*. The programme changed the televisual landscape of the 1990s and had Lovejoy & Co. introducing wacky features such as 'Can he kick it?', 'The Nutmeg Files' and 'Crossbar Challenge'. He then set about the studio audience with a giant rubber mallet.

There was the Pankhurst-inspired 'Soccerette' feature. Each week a glamorous young lady was paraded in front of the studio audience dressed in hot-pants and a skimpy *Soccer AM* T-shirt. But it was okay, 'cos it was irony, wasn't it? And the T-shirt wasn't actually wet.

Soccer AM's contribution to gender equality didn't finish there – there was the whole 'Save Chip' phenomenon. Some bloke called Chip was told he couldn't watch football any more by his girlfriend. Lovejoy took the campaign to the streets and before long a bloodless coup saw Tim installed as Prime Minister and a raunchy image of Chip's missus projected on to the side of the Houses of Parliament.*

By the late 1990s, it was clear that Lovejoy was controlling every facet of world football from the comfort of his *Soccer AM* armchair. It was Tim's idea to get a gold star superglued onto England's kit in recognition of something or other achieved in the 1960s.

Anyway, most of Lovejoy's achievements have been relayed to us second-hand. As we've said before, we don't have Sky TV, so we can't be 100 per cent sure that any of the above is actually true. We first stumbled across Tim when he took over *606* on BBC Radio 5 Live and that's when it became clear to us that Tim was personally to blame for all of the modern game's ills. *606* has suffered from its fair share of dodgy presenters: David Mellor (another Chelsea fan; it can't be coincidence, can it?) did much to undo the good work done by original host Danny Baker; while Dominik Diamond and Richard Littlejohn's stints in the presenter's chair further tested the show's credibility; but Lovejoy took the programme to new depths.

We're not quite sure what it was – his overt Chelsea bias, the fact that he appeared to be best mates with every footballer ever mentioned on the show, or his attitude to callers who had the cheek to phone in about anything other than the Premiership. The awfulness of his Wednesday night show was compounded by the return of Danny Baker to *606* the night before. Baker's shows are crammed full of irreverent, intelligent humour and even the callers seem to be funnier. From the sublime to the ridiculous in 24 hours.

So here's the thing: most people we know have the same opinion of Lovejoy. As a consequence we assumed that *everyone* felt the same. Imagine our surprise leafing through

Facebook when we discovered hundreds of groups devoted to Tim. The largest of these groups, 'Bring Back Tim Lovejoy to *Soccer AM*', has more than 9,000,000 members – not all of them can be disgruntled *606* listeners.

So, it looks like we were wrong. Tim is loved and loathed in almost equal measure. Furthermore, it seems Lovejoy packing his bags and returning to *Soccer AM* would make everyone happy. Over to you, Tim.

* We might be getting confused here. It could equally have been Gail Porter who became Prime Minister and Tony Blair whose scantily clad image was projected onto the walls of Westminster Palace.

Mansize rooster

How many times have you thought to yourself that you could do better than the latest shower-of-shit that's out there representing your club? And how many times have you said that you'd gladly play for free?

Trouble is, it's an empty gesture – if you are anything like us you were always too fat, slow and crap to ever be selected. The gulf between Premier and Sunday League was so great that your altruism was never in danger of being put to the test.

Playing for free? It does happen, usually when a lower-league club are in financial trouble and the staff carry on without pay for several weeks. It's admirable, but is a response to dire circumstances rather than something initiated by the players. It could also be argued that in a bid to get to the 2010 World Cup David Beckham played for free at AC Milan. Not strictly true, but it is rumoured that Becks took a substantial pay cut to go on loan to Milan and also greased the wheels with a financial contribution from his own personal fortune. Again, admirable on Becks' part, but ultimately an act fuelled by professional desire.

But one man is playing for free – and for all the right reasons. Athletic Bilbao winger Joseba Etxeberria is playing the entire 2009/10 season for free. Yep, nada.

Etxeberria, known as 'The Rooster' by virtue of his long neck, has been at the club for his entire 15-year career. Joseba said of his decision to play for free; 'This is a thank-you to the behaviour of the club towards me and the love I have received from so many people.' It is certainly an act of ultimate loyalty. But it was nearly so different. 'The Rooster' began his love affair with Athletic Bilbao by ruffling a few feathers in San Sebastián – he joined the club as a 17-year-old from local rivals Real Sociedad in controversial circumstances – and Bilbao ended up paying more than 3 million euros for the young winger. This 'betrayal' has never been forgotten by fans at the Estadio Anoeta.

Athletic Bilbao – who pride themselves on fielding only Basque-born players – are forever grateful to Etxeberria, with president Fernando Garcia Macua gushing: 'From the club's standpoint there are not words enough to thank such a gesture.' And he's probably right. It is a noble gesture, and an idea that we hope catches on. Think of it as a reverse testimonial – a thank you to the club that has shaped a player's life. It would be nice to think that any club benefiting from a similar gesture would reinvest the money saved in wages into their youth structure – thus making the circle complete.

Ashley Cole take note. This was a man-size gesture from the señor they call 'The Rooster'.

Matchday magazine

When did the humble football programme become a sodding 'matchday magazine'? And when did they start charging upwards of £3 for the privilege?

The original purpose of a football programme was to tell you the team line-ups for the match in question: a simple, single-sided affair, churned out of a John Bull printing press on the morning of the match. If you were lucky, you might get an advert for the local ironmonger tucked away at the bottom of the sheet.

Now, you sure as hell don't get the team line-ups, just two squad lists that are more like a facsimile of the latest population census, rather than a simple teamsheet.

But these aren't football programmes. No, they are matchday magazines, an example of one of those horrible, aspirational alliterations – like the effin' credit crunch... Hmmm, 'credit crunch', you say? Sounds tasty. What do you mean, we've all lost our jobs, homes and life savings? Likewise, the matchday magazine is just some marketing gimp's attempt to rebrand 36 pages of adverts, advertorials and bland ghostwritten columns. Who do they think they're kidding? We've just spent our last three quid on this, err, magazine, we don't want to sponsor Tom Huddlestone's socks, or buy an executive luncheon package for two. Sorry.

Now, while we are on the subject of alliterations, whatever happened to 'Golden Goal' tickets?

Military tattoos

Tattoos used to be the exclusive preserve of soldiers, sailors and the criminally insane. After drinking themselves stupid on three days shore-leave, service personnel would inevitably find themselves in some grubby backstreet basement getting a tattoo. Well, it was either that or the local knocking shop (the chance of contracting something nasty was much the same with either option).

Back then, no matter where you were in the world, there were only three or four possibilities when it came to getting a tattoo. You could have a heart, a dagger, an anchor, a snake, or any combination of the above inked onto your forearm. Underneath, you were legally obliged to have 'Mum' tattooed in a fancy scripted font. That was pretty much it. Although, slide a few dollars under the counter, and you might be able to persuade the sweaty bloke with the needle to tattoo 'Love' and 'Hate' in between the knuckles on your hands. Nice.

Now, every footballer from David Beckham to some bloke in the reserves at Carlisle is covered in tattoos. Not old school ones either.

No, today, your average footballer will start by getting the legend 'Darren' etched on the inside of his arm *in Sanskrit*. Then, there's the obligatory Che Guevara tattoo on the top of an arm (99% of footballers haven't got a clue who Guevara was, which is just as well as their tattoo usually ends up looking like a poor photostat of Micky Droy in his Chelsea heyday).

By now the player is on a roll, and he will usually go for the BIG ONE: the Crucifixion scene across the shoulders and down the back. This, he reckons, makes him look spiritual and never fails to impress in a three-in-a-hot-tub situation.

To finish off, the player will add the name of his children, pet or current girlfriend to the base of his spine. That used to be it, but recently we've noticed that a number of high-profile players have decided to cover their entire arms with a complex mish-mash of tattoos – from the wrist up to the sleeve of their T-shirt. The effect is a bizarre sort of reverse tank-top look.

Modern footballers and tattoos – not an anchor in sight. But plenty of wankers.

Missing links

As kids there was nothing greater than discovering a vaguely personal link to a famous player. Never mind that six degrees of separation rubbish; we are talking proper, bona fide links. There were two principal ways: first, through a name; and second, through a birthday. Names were easy, but it was harder to obtain birthdays in the days before Google. Newspapers often listed people born on a particular day in their horoscope section, which at least gave us reason to stop and gaze at the stars before heading for Miriam's Photo Casebook.

In order to fully understand these tenuous links to the footballing greats, we need to let Shaun slip into first-person vernacular...

When I was growing up the main 'Hunt' on the scene was Steve Hunt of Coventry City. I followed his career, not knowing I would end up studying in Coventry just a couple of miles from Highfield Road. It would have been out of this world to find a professional footballer sharing my full name, but at least Steve had the same first initial. He even won two England caps under Bobby Robson. But what was the best thing about Steve Hunt? No, not the classic Midlands moustache he wore in his early days, but the fact that I could sign 'S. Hunt' on *Football Manager* and pretend he was me! Always my first signing, Steve was an ever present in the great *Football Manager* teams of my youth. Captain as well. He was my rock.

Just when I thought being a Hunt couldn't get any better, Roy Race went and signed ace midfielder Carl 'The Hunter' Hunt for the mighty Melchester Rovers. I could have danced all night. Some might cruelly point out that on the team sheet he was C. Hunt with a silent 'H' – but I didn't care; us Hunts have had to put up with rhymes like that all our lives. Unfortunately for Carl he looked like a German porn-star, but, luckily, I didn't know about such things at the time. Hunt had signed for Rovers after starring in a six-a-side tournament. Yet, tragedy lurked for my distant relative: in 1986, only two years after signing, Carl died in the middle-east principality of Basran, after a bungled terrorist attack which killed seven other players. I was distraught. Steve Hunt's career was winding down and 'The Hunter' had become the hunted. It was a sad time for the Hunt dynasty. Of course, there was always Roger (who I hoped I was related to). Having a World Cup winner in the 'family', was great, but he was from a different era. And, although he'd played for Liverpool, he couldn't compete with Carl and Steve. Similarly, I am sorry to admit that Stephen and Noel Hunt do absolutely nothing for me – I'm sure they will be really upset by that admission.

As for birthdays, well, I had an absolute legend sharing my special day. We all hoped there was some cosmic link that would guarantee footballing greatness if a superstar shared our birthday. I was lucky: the late, great Brian Clough was also born on 21st March. I would like to believe I shared much of his genius, but I have so far failed to win even one European Cup. Cloughie was an enigma, and by writing about him, I am hoping to cash in on his genius like the other 576 other books about him that are on the market. While I can't pretend to have been a huge fan of Clough, I admired him and was pleased to tell everyone he shared my birthday. Unfortunately, no one gave a toss.

The relationship between fans and their idols is a very personal affair, which means nothing to anyone else. On realising this you also realise that you are not the centre of the universe, and that everyone has different and justified opinions. Man, growing up can be tough.

While researching this article, I discovered that Lothar Matthaus and Ronald Koeman also share my birthday. I had not uncovered this link previously, because I don't recall either of them making it into the *Daily Mirror's* birthday list.

Looking back, I am glad, because both have been England's nemesis at some point. However, I would like you to know that the fantastically gifted and physically attractive Ronaldinho also shares my birthday. Make of that what you will.

So there you have it, a name or birthday could be the missing link between you and footballing greatness – it's also a good excuse to dwell on the horoscope page of your favourite paper.

By way of a postscript, Nick is always banging on about his birthday being the day after that of his all-time hero, John Barnes. Apparently, this makes them both moody Scorpios, and devilishly good with their left peg. Until recently, Nick has struggled to find any football-playing Davidsons, saddled instead with an ex-Doctor Who and a dodgy 'comedian'. But, in the last season or so, Nick's adopted club FC St. Pauli of Hamburg gave a debut to a young player called Davidson Drobo-Ampem. Nick nearly wet himself when he found out, and is currently saving all proceeds from this book to go towards having 'Drobo-Cop's' (inspired nickname, eh?) full name on the back of a shirt.

Mitchell and Webb

We're starting to feel old and vulnerable. When someone told us that Mitchell and Webb had been signed up to front the British version of the legendary 'Get a Mac' adverts we were confused. Thoroughly.

As Apple Mac devotees we'd chortled along at the American version of these adverts on the internet. If you haven't seen them, a hip, young 20-something with great hair is the personal embodiment of an Apple Mac, while a geeky bloke with glasses and an ill-fitting suit represents a PC with – as they say – hilarious consequences!

But why had Apple opted to cast a couple of '80s footballers in the UK version of the advert? The lightly-bearded Dave Mitchell had a brief moment in the sun playing for a Glenn Hoddle inspired Swindon Town in their dramatic 1993 Play-Off final win over Leicester City, but after a couple of seasons with Millwall it all went quiet.

Then there was Neil Webb of Nottingham Forest, Manchester United and England, yet best remembered as the husband of Shelley – a journalist and television presenter who came to our attention presenting the under-rated football magazine show *Standing Room Only*.

So what of this revival? True, one had a stylish beard and the other TV connections, but it still seemed unlikely that in the intervening years they'd done enough to secure a lucrative advertising deal? Then we found out about the stand-up comedy, the successful television and radio show and the film. Wowza – as far as we could work out Mitchell and Webb had never even played in the same team (Webb did have a brief loan spell at Swindon in 1994, but Mitchell had already fled, migrating to Turkey).

Then it dawned on us. It wasn't *that* Mitchell and Webb. Doh! How stupid are we? Turns out the real Dave Mitchell is now managing Perth Glory in the Australian A-League, while

Neil Webb had a spell as a postie (good on yer Neil, we love our postmen*) before working at Charlton.

That'll teach us.

*That's genuine sincerity by the way. We fully support the posties – they do a grand job and get very little thanks and a lot of unnecessary criticism.

Modern footballs are rubbish

It's not just kits that change every bloody season. It's balls too. And a World Cup or European Championship offers further scope to fiddle with football's most vital equipment. Manufacturers routinely proclaim that their latest offering is rounder, faster, lighter and infinitely more attractive to the opposite sex. How can this be? Essentially a football is a football – bits of leather stitched together and pumped full of air. We can understand that things evolve; for instance a football no longer requires external laces to hold it together, and thus diddy, Brylcreemed wingers in impossibly long shorts are no longer required to deliver said ball onto the No. 9's head 'lace side up'.

And we appreciate that at some point during the last 40 years, boffins worked out how to make a ball waterproof, effectively ending the practice of trying to hoof a cannon-ball through slurry, as was the case for most of the 1950s, '60s and early '70s. But once you've made it waterproof and ditched the laces, any further improvements can only be cosmetic, can't they? Apparently not.

Footballs continue to evolve and mutate at a speed usually reserved for Swine Flu. Each time a new ball is unleashed, it is heralded by a load of technical psychobabble: out goes 'stitching' and in comes 'thermal bonding'; while 'three-layer syntactic foam knitted chassis' becomes *de rigueur* (and no, we haven't got a clue what any of that means, either).

In 2006, balls did seem to take a bit of an evolutionary leap forwards, with Adidas launching the 'Teamgeist' matchball at the World Cup in Germany. Out went the traditional 32 panels and in came 14 curved panels. The upshot of this great leap forward? Yup, you guessed it – the roundest football ever. The Wikipedia description uses language lifted directly from the GSCE maths curriculum: 'The Teamgeist ball differs from previous balls in having just 14 curved panels making the ball topologically equivalent to a truncated octa-hedron.' Glad we cleared that up.

Although balls are changing all the time, the big ad-vances are usually reserved for World Cup years. Yet these supposed progressions have provided us with some unusual curios.

First, we all just *know* that the ball used in England's 4-2 win over Germany in the 1966 World Cup final was bright orange – strange considering that the majority of the popu-lation were watching the match at home on black and white television. Most football fans also know that it took a high-profile media campaign from those plucky boys (and girls) at the *Daily Mirror* to get the ball back from Helmut Haller, who scored West Germany's first goal in the 1966 final, and managed to hang on to the ball for 30 years (Helmut handed it over to England in 1996).

Second, the 1970 World Cup in Mexico was the first to be broadcast in glorious technicolour, yet Adidas chose this occasion to introduce the 'Telstar' matchball – essentially a white ball with black panels. We can't help thinking that the balls from the '66 and '70 World Cups would've been better employed the other way round – and are the perfect subject for a future episode of *Doctor Who* if ever we saw one.

As kids, it was the balls used in the World Cup that we craved. Every youngster growing up in the 1970s or '80s yearned for an Adidas 'Telstar' or its successor, the iconic 'Tango'. Some of us even went so far as to draw 'Tango' markings on the balls we bought from Woolies.

Strangely, those cheap plastic balls we bought with our pocket money seems to be where the modern-day match ball is heading. With every advance, footballs seem to get lighter and more unpredictable, drawing exasperated groans from goalkeepers everywhere. Perhaps that's what the world's leading scientists have been doing in that tunnel deep beneath the Franco-Swiss border – they are not trying to collide atoms, in search of the elusive Higgs boson particle – no, they are trying to recreate the equally illusive 'double-swerve', last achieved by kids in the 1970s with one of those 99p plastic footballs. You remember? The blast with the outside of the foot that would cause your ball to viciously swerve first one way then the other, totally bamboozling the poor sod in goal (take one of these lightweight balls to the beach on a windy day and you quite feasibly break every law of physics in the book).

These new balls might be rounder, faster and lighter but we can't help thinking it's a classic case of the 'Emperor's New Balls' – and that we'd be much better off playing with a cheap plastic football from Menzies or Woolworths.

Modern footballs? They're just rubbish.

More than three Sheikhs...

We can't help thinking that more than three Sheikhs in the Premier League... is a really bad idea.

Not a week goes by without another foreign trillionaire buying up a Premiership club. Russian oligarchs, oilmen from Texas to Saudi Arabia – all desperate to pay over the odds for mid-table obscurity.

At first, it was quite exciting. Roman Abramovich at Chelsea hoovering up big-name signings like Florentino Pérez on *Supermarket Sweep*. Then Sheikh Mansour Bin Zayed Al Nahyan bought Manchester City and things started to get out of hand. The Abu Dhabi United Group took control of City on 1st September 2008, transfer deadline day, and set about trying to hijack Dimitar Berbatov's move to Manchester United. It didn't work, but they did land Real Madrid misfit Robinho for a British record £32.5 million. The scattergun transfer policy continued in the January window, with City reportedly willing to pay £100 million to bring Kaka to Eastlands. It failed and City ended up with Craig Bellamy.

Make no mistake, these cash-rich owners are only interested in *your* club because it buys them kudos, because the Premier League is this year's plaything-*célèbre*. We are just bitter, secretly wishing that a previously unknown Uzbekistani cotton magnate would pump billions into our club, delivering league titles aplenty.

Then again, we'd wager that your average Chelsea fan would swap all their recent silverware for another chance to see John Bumstead in his pomp. Winning the Premier League is all well and good, but it is never going to rival the thrill of Chelsea's dramatic 5-4 win over Man City in the 1986 Full Members Cup, something both Abramovich and the Sheikhy-fella at Man City would do well to remember.

We realise we are straying into *Daily Mail* country, but we long for the days when our football clubs were owned by good, honest, *British* businessmen. Industrialists or entrepreneurs with integrity; local lads made good; men like Robert Maxwell or Stan Flashman.

As we said at the start, more than three Sheikhs is a… *(look, they got it the first time, okay? – Ed.)*

Moveable feasts

Oh, the uproar. Oh, the irony. UEFA have moved the Champions League final from a Wednesday to a Saturday night. The reaction to this decision has been astounding – football is up in arms. Tony Woodcock – former European Cup winner and possibly the only Englishman to play for both 1.FC Köln and Fortuna Köln – was nothing short of furious when *FourFourTwo* magazine tackled him on the subject: 'Doesn't feel right... I prefer to stick to tradition and have the final played during the week. Whether it's a bad idea or not I don't know, but I don't like it.' Quite, Tony, quite.

How dare UEFA tinker so thoughtlessly with 'tradition'. There's a very real danger that the competition's integrity will be called into question.

Whatever next... Qualification skewed in favour of Europe's big leagues? A laborious group stage? The same three or four (English) teams in the semi-finals ever year? You are right, Tony, it's the European Cup, but not as we know it.

There must be some sinister masterplan behind the switch and it probably involves increased television revenue, bigger sponsorship and a nicer buffet, but Platini says he's doing it for the kids (of course), and we're with him every step of the way. Having the final on a Saturday is great – as long as it doesn't interfere with *Strictly*.

Actually, Michel, could you get on the blower to Sepp Blatter and get the World Cup final shifted to a Saturday too? Sunday nights belong to *Last of the Summer Wine*.

My balls have dropped

Every so often as kids there was a time when no one knew what to do in a game of football. The general rule of thumb was that there had to be a drop, or bounce ball. No one knew the precise rules or exactly why we did it. Even in official matches the referees didn't seem sure.

The usual reason for this type of restart was an injury. After an injury, everyone stood around. Then, after an uncomfortable pause, the referee would shout, 'bounce ball' or 'drop ball'. There seemed to be no consistency as to whether the ball was going to be dropped or bounced. We knew no better, so were happy to go along with the man in black.

Regardless of where the incident had occurred on the pitch the restart always ended up on the centre spot. Again we never knew if this was correct, FA-endorsed procedure. We rarely saw it on *Match of the Day* or *The Big Match*, and, as far as we can recall, it had never been sketched out in *You Are The Ref* either.

A player from each side was then chosen. In kids' football these players fell into two distinct categories.

First choice was the best player, invariably the manager's son – known as the Dennis Waterman of the team, because he did absolutely everything. He might've been the obvious choice, but there was one alternative.

Every team had a hard player. He wasn't necessarily a good footballer, but he was on the team because everyone was scared to boot him out. Blessed with a hard shot and a mean tackle as well as being dead handy in a post-match fight, he stalked the penalty area waiting for a forward to wander into his territory. For a drop ball his talents were perfect, and here's why.

Despite being called a 'drop' ball, it was rare that the ball actually *dropped* any great distance. As soon as it left the referee's hand the race to strike the ball was on. If the ball was released from too great a height, a kung-fu kick was the natural conclusion. Of course, this was a dangerous manoeuvre that could result in injury for both players and the referee.

Regardless of the height from which the referee dropped the ball, the restart always descended into something from the *Ultimate Fight Championship*. If a player missed the ball, he had time to reposition himself and aim a crafty kick at his opponent before the referee realised what was going on. Sometimes the ball would become trapped between the players and the referee, resulting in a multiple pile-up.

Smarter managers soon got wise to this free-for-all and would not risk their best player in a drop ball situation, and this made the team hard man the obvious choice.

If the referee made the mistake of calling for a bounce ball, the restart could take as long as five minutes. Asking two kids to watch a ball to bounce before kicking it was like asking them to not breathe. It could not be done. The possibility of letting the opposition gain an advantage would prove too much every time. The ball would be struck countless times before it hit the floor, resulting in the referee having to start all over again. Add to this scenario the two toughest kids on the park not wanting to be outgunned by the other and you've got a recipe for disaster. Last time we looked, the record for attempting to restart a game from a bounce ball stands at 47 bounces. On a still night, the echo of shin clashing against shin resonates around council recs up and down the country – the crunching sound of bone on bone providing a ghostly backdrop for late-night dog walkers.

Compare this with today: the ball is given back to the opposition as a gesture of goodwill, which results in clapping all round. Where's the fun in that? Bring back the real bounce ball with real kicks, real competition and the real possibility the referee could get hurt.

No Ball Games Allowed

Ever wondered why we haven't won a World Cup in more than 40 years? The answer is simple: it's due to the idiots at the council who stick 'No Ball Games Allowed' signs on every available patch of grass.

These signs sum up everything that is wrong with British culture. They are put there to appease a few middle-class curtain twitchers who can't bear to have their Sunday afternoons spoiled by oiks playing football on the green outside their houses – it lowers the tone of the neighbourhood and a stray ball might damage their precious rhododendrons. Guess what, Reg and Maureen? These 'oiks' are much less likely to stab you, if you let them entertain themselves playing football.

Banning kids from playing football in public places just facilitates a downward spiral that contributes to the (largely imagined) moral decay currently scaring the living daylights out of your average *Daily Mail* reader.

Let them play football and shoplifting, drug use and muggings will disappear overnight. Give 'em a ball and a yard of grass and 'The Kids' will probably even help you across the road. We'll also stand a chance of winning the World Cup.

Can you imagine a similar 'No Ball Games' scenario in Argentina or Brazil? Here are two nations where every scrap of waste ground has a set of goalposts. Okay, the crime level in the favelas doesn't quite support our 'more football, less violence' hypothesis, but Argentina and Brazil have seven World Cup wins between them, so they must be doing something right.

So, let's rise up against this insipid council bureaucracy. We couldn't possibly suggest that you just ignore the signage, but we strongly urge you to write to your local district councillor insisting they take down the signs and replace them with a set of goalposts – if they question the political mileage, remind them of Harold Wilson and the World Cup afterglow; that should seal the deal.

Nouveaux riches

Back in the 1970s you could count the names of celebrity fans on the digits of one hand. You had Eric Morecambe supporting Luton; Elton John down the road at Watford; TV funnymen Stan Boardman and Jimmy Tarbuck both following Liverpool; Rod Stewart supporting Scotland. And that was it.

Now, everyone from Atomic Kitten's Liz McClarnon (Everton) to Bubble from *Big Brother 2* (Chelsea, more of that later) find it necessary to make public their support for a particular team. It never used to be like this, but then again during the 1970s and '80s football just wasn't cool. Even comic book flirtations with celebrity failed to stretch the imagination: the best *Roy of the Rovers* could offer us was Spandau Ballet's Gary and Martin Kemp on the pitch (why?) and Geoff Boycott and Simon Mayo in the boardroom (not at the same time we might add; that would have been too much!).

It must be a combination of football's increased popularity and the country's obsession with fame that has seen this unholy union of football club and minor celebrity spread like wildfire through the nation's gossip pages. There is no turning the tide. Naming your football club is as integral to being a celebrity as selling your wedding photos to *Hello!*

No club is immune from this disease – from Torquay (Helen Chamberlain) in the south-west to Hartlepool (Peter Mandelson and Jeff Stelling) in the north-east – but one club stands head and shoulders above the rest when it comes to 'celebrity' supporters. That club is Chelsea.

Of course, Chelsea's glamorous King's Road location means they've always been a convenient stopping-off point for stars hungry for a photo-opportunity. In the 1960s and '70s, Steve McQueen and Raquel Welch were rumoured to have had tours of the Chelsea dressing room – the very thought of catching a glimpse of Chopper Harris in his jock-strap too much of an opportunity to turn down, we'd imagine. Then, during the 1980s celebs were often found queuing outside the West Stand at all hours just for the chance to snuggle up to Ken Bates in the Chelsea directors' box. But this was a transient popularity. You couldn't call these people fans, just celebrity tourists with tight media schedules and even tighter trousers.

It was the arrival of Abramovich, money and – some co-incidence this – trophies at Stamford Bridge that started to see famous fans flock to the Bridge in their droves. It was a Diana Ross (unattached), probably can't even look at a football after the USA 94 opening ceremony debacle-style chain reaction: money buys success, attracts celebrity liggers.

Yep, Chelsea is probably the only club in the country with a waiting list for celebrity fans. You can't even go for a pee at Stamford Bridge without bumping into Guy Ritchie or Simon Pegg.

The Chelsea website even publishes a list of famous fans. At the last count there were 165 names from the worlds of cinema, television, music, sport, journalism, politics, miscellaneous (inc. Vidal Sassoon and Aldo Zilli) and a section listing famous Chelsea fans who have departed this mortal coil.

But one name is absent from this list. On a Saturday morning not so long ago, we were sitting in the car on the way to a far-flung away game, listening to Radio 5 Live when Jeremy Clarkson revealed to Eamonn Holmes (Manchester United, see Holmes advantage) that he was – yep, you guessed it – a Chelsea fan.

As if Mellor, Major and Lovejoy weren't bad enough. Jeremy Clarkson, a committed petrol-head and unfathomably successful author (jealous, us?) – who had never before expressed a public interest in the game we love – follows Chelsea.

We imagine Clarkson's revelation will go down in history as 'the day that football died'.

Odd job

Q. How many Manchester United players does it take to change a light bulb?

A. None – a bloke called Barry does it for them.

You thought Manchester United's recent domestic (domestic, geddit?) success was all down to Fergie? Think again. It's club 'fixer' Barry Moorhouse's retirement United should be planning for – casting a net far and wide for an odd-job man with anywhere near the same panache as Bazza.

The press had a field day when United defender Patrice Evra blabbed about the lives of the stars. The *Daily Mirror* quoted pampered Patrice thus: 'You can ask Barry anything. When you have a problem with your car, the Jacuzzi or the light, he is there.' A club source responded: 'United have players from all over the world and it can be difficult for them to settle.' Yes, because changing a light bulb in a foreign language is a tricky business.

We really shouldn't be surprised by this degree of pampering; after all, our footballers have been wrapped up in cotton wool for years. What is surprising is that United's superstars have to *share* Barry between them. You'd think they'd want one each.

With this in mind, perhaps further education establishments in the north-west are missing a trick – they should seriously consider running a GNVQ in the domestic and electrical needs of professional footballers. The modules are easy to break down: term one – changing light bulbs; term two – fixing Jacuzzis; term three – putting new batteries in the remote control that opens the electronic gates.

For what it's worth, Barry is remarkably stoic about it all: 'Some people describe me as a Jim'll Fix It,' which is fine, except in our heads he was less like Jimmy Savile and more akin to Goldfinger's henchman, Oddjob – a fixer in more ways than one. Sure, he can stop Wayne Rooney's fridge door squeaking, but if requested by Fergie he could also dispatch a particularly annoying linesman with his metal-rimmed bowler – now that's a proper handyman.

One hundred million dollar match, the

Apparently, the Championship (that's Division Two in old money) Play-Off final is the most important match in world football. Yep, the chance to spend a season in the top flight – on the wrong end of spankings from everyone including Aston Villa and Everton – before inevitable confirmation of relegation the following March, is far more important than, say, winning the World Cup.

But it's not really about the football, is it? It's all about the wonga. Every season four clubs get a VIP pass to a post-season casino – football's very own Sunset Strip – where they put their chips on the table for the chance to grab a place in the Premier League.

By the time four clubs are whittled down to two, and a showpiece Wembley final, the media have gone into overdrive. The match is dubbed as a 'winner takes all' showdown. Crazy numbers are bandied about; it used to be £30 million; then it was £60 million. Now Championship Play-Off winners are on the receiving end of an unsubstantiated '£100 million cash bonanza'. Nobody is quite sure how this sum is calculated, least of all the tabloid hacks who worked it out on the back of a fag packet. Telly money, increased sponsorship revenue and global branding opportunities are bandied about and the figure is blithely accepted and regurgitated as fact on TV and radio.

We can't help thinking these newly promoted clubs should be more careful with their money. If they really do trouser anything like £100 million, then how the hell have Leeds, Leicester, Norwich and Southampton (who've all had the keys to the Premiership bank-vault in recent years) found themselves doing time in football's third tier?

The reality is twofold: first, winning the Play-Offs doesn't net anywhere near £100 million; and second the rag-tag ensemble of second-rate footballers that somehow achieved promotion now think they are superstars and demand – via their equally vile agents – ridiculous pay-rises for the honour of representing their side in the top flight. Factor in a couple of expensive and ill-advised foreign signings and that's the money up in smoke. You almost wonder why clubs bother.

Origins of symmetry

Football kits should be as plain as possible. If they have to have any stylistic accoutrements, then simple stripes on the sleeves, down the side of the shorts, or around the top of the socks should do it. The excellent 2009/11 England shirt is a case in point – so simple it could be a £2.99 polo shirt from Primark (giving you the option to just buy a polo shirt and get your mum to sew the badge on – it's what we used to do as kids).

Sadly, needlework is a dying art, and so too are simplistic football shirts. As the 1970s became the '80s we got used to pin-stripes and contra-shadows (Spurs home '82) and we just about survived the acid casualty designs of the early 1990s (Arsenal away '91), but now kit manufacturers have clobbered us with asymmetrical kit designs.

Everyone is at it, from the big boys at Adidas to the smaller manufacturers making kits for one or two clubs. At some point in the last five years, designers took leave of their senses and decided that it would be a good idea to design stupid shirts with asymmetrical patterns. You know the sort of thing: a contrasting coloured shoulder swoosh on one side, or just one white sleeve with the other sleeve remaining green (and yes, Plymouth Argyle 2009/10, we mean you!).

Sure, fashion moves on and, sure, kit designers are trying to reach out to 'da kidz', but they'd do well to remember that it's us – middle-aged men – who make up the largest demographic in the replica shirt market. And we don't want to wander round town on a Saturday morning looking like an extra from *Dancing on Ice*.

Asymmetry isn't even all that new. It was done, somewhat less extravagantly in the late 1970s. Plenty of teams opted for the vertical stripe down one side of the shirt – perhaps the most famous exponent of this genre being Melchester Rovers – a plain red top with a single tasteful yellow stripe on the front. You had the feeling Roy Race could get away with wearing any old clobber, but Scottish hard-man, Duncan McKay, wouldn't have been seen dead in a shirt that made him look like Robin Cousins. The Melchester Rovers strip goes down as a design classic, while today's motley array of shirts should be confined to the dustbin of history.

Hopefully these lame asymmetrical kit designs are just a passing fad, and soon we'll be back to the day-glo, paint-splattered monstrosities of the early 1990s. We can live in hope.

The bottom line is this... football kits need to be symmetrical. Leave the fancy stuff for the ice rink. Whatever next? Sequins?

Partisan ballboys

What ever happened to partisan ballboys?

Every goal scored in the 1970s was greeted with an explosion of pure joy from the tracksuit-clad youths behind the goal. Check old *Match of the Day* videos and, from Ashton Gate to Stamford Bridge, you'll see ballboys leaping about, hugging each other every time the ball gets bundled over the line. It was a teenage adrenalin-rush that, if properly harnessed, could have provided a genuine alternative to fossil fuels.

Occasionally, the actual goalscorer would stray into that patch of muddy wasteland behind the goal only to be engulfed by a crazed mob of snotty-nosed ballboys. It was a joy to watch.

Today, as a player, you'd consider yourself lucky if the disinterested teenager masquerading as a ballboy stopped texting his mates, got up from his plastic stool and actually gave you the ball back. They sure as hell aren't going to celebrate with you. It's just not cool to show emotion. A last-minute winner – belted home from 35 yards – in a cup semi-final? Bothered?

Pen pictures

Like steeplejacks, thatchers (note the lower-case 't') and lacemakers, writers of 'pen pictures' in your matchday programme are a dying breed.

You remember pen pictures. You remember them because, aside from the manager's (ghostwritten) notes and the league tables, they were the only thing worth reading in your programme – the only thing worth the scandalous 25 pence you'd paid the doddery old chap with the leather satchel, who'd been hawking them outside the ground since the dawn of time.

Before the internet, satellite TV and glossy full-colour matchday magazines (see Matchday magazines) the only way to find out anything about the opposition's centre forward was to read his pen pic in the programme. If you were really lucky, or the striker was particularly well known, you might get a grainy black and white portrait of the player, but mostly you relied on the pen picture.

Pen pictures were either written by a local journalist (earning a bit of extra wedge moonlighting for the club), or they'd be penned by the programme editor himself (who usually doubled as the club secretary). Either way they were never very informative. They'd contain a few sketchy facts, about where a player was born and what clubs he'd played for previously. Editors wouldn't risk anything current or controversial and, as a result, you'd rarely have a clue as to how many goals the bloke had scored that season. Often the information was so hopelessly out of date that much of the squad had moved on (this was especially common at the start of the season, when the programme editor would simply recycle last year's effort).

But, however out of date or woefully inaccurate, the description of a player in his pen pic was *the law*. Terrace arguments about an opponent could be stopped dead in their tracks with confirmation from the bloke a few steps down with a match programme. If it said a player once went on loan to Torquay United in the programme, then he went on loan to them – end of argument.

By the beginning of the 1980s we suspected something was awry in the world of pen pics – and that was syndication. On our travels around, we started to see similarities in players' descriptions that suggested something was wrong. A closed circle of journalists seemed to be trading pen pics and the result meant you'd be reading pretty much the same thing every week. It was the beginning of the end.

Now, of course, Bread's prophecy has come to pass and 'a picture does indeed paint a thousand words'. As a result programmes are packed with glossy photos of the away team in action and pen pics have been replaced by up-to-the-minute statistical analysis.

It's a shame. There was something almost mystical about knowing that Brian Greenhalgh was born in Chesterfield and started his career at Preston North End – knowing any more seemed both unnecessary and invasive.

Perfect penalty, my arse

We are fed up with commentators proclaiming virtually every penalty that goes in as 'perfect'.

The main one that really pisses us off is when the ball nestles in the corner of the net and the commentator glibly proclaims, 'It is right in the corner of the net. Perfect positioning.'

No, it's not 'perfect bloody positioning!' It's not perfect, because the corner of the net is NOT the corner of the goal. The corner of the goal is just inside each post. So if the ball is nestling in the corner of the net it is not f*****g perfect. It's not difficult. It is simple. If you are going to state the obvious, at least know what you are talking about.

Secondly, the goalkeeper can move. So, even if you hit the perfect penalty just inside the post, or maybe hitting the post on the way in (even more perfect?), the goalkeeper could have already moved towards that post and actually be in a position to save it. In this case, it would not have been a perfect penalty.

A perfect penalty depends on a number of factors, but there are only two outcomes that matter: the player either scores or he doesn't. Simple as that.

Pierless

You might have spotted that we've decided to wage war on celebrity fans. Although, when we say 'war' we really mean a half-hearted assault, as the royalties we receive from this book don't run to employing a full-time team of shit-hot libel lawyers.

Anyway, back to the case in hand: imagine our surprise, when Nick's mum brought round a copy of *The Mail on Sunday's* football supplement. The fact that she left the rest of the *Mail* at home is proof that she still possesses some of her faculties. She didn't want to ruin another Sunday afternoon with a rant about her choice of newspaper (she only buys it for the TV guide, honest). And what could possibly be upsetting about a football supplement, eh? Nothing much. Well, not until we got to the very last page.

You see, Piers Morgan has bagged himself a weekly full-page opinion piece. Apparently he likes football. A search on Google also revealed he spent a whole year with Arsenal in 2003/04, and enjoyed it so much he wrote a book, *Va Va Voom!* about it. To think we'd had him nailed as another pesky nouveau fan.

To be fair to Piers, we are never going to see eye-to-eye with him. He's a judge on *Britain's Got Talent* and we are a couple of deluded middle-aged wasters. But ask yourself this: does football really need another celebrity columnist?

It is time strict criteria were imposed for those writing about the game we love. We can't really argue with ex-pros, no matter how inarticulate, as they've been there, done it and got the drink problem (and a half-decent ghostwriter can usually tease out some vaguely interesting opinion), but this flurry of minor celebrities writing about football is just getting embarrassing.

If you are going to write about football on a regular basis, we'll need evidence that you are not some Johnny Come

Lately, media luvvy who got into the game when it became sexy (widely acknowledged to coincide with Ruud Gullit's arrival at Chelsea in 1995). We want to see scrapbooks from when you were a kid, or blurry photographs of your eight-year-old self, clinging desperately to Malcolm Macdonald's sideburns on the steps of Highbury. Think of it as a football-related CRB check; we'll call it a JCL check (or Johnny Come Lately). If you can't produce the evidence, bugger off back to Hampstead.

And don't fret about the empty column inches. We've got the scrapbooks, we've done our time on the terraces (and, yes, we mean *terraces*, not the comfy padded seats in the main stand) and we are happy to opine on all things football for a fraction of the money. So, who's it to be – Piers Stefan Pughe-Morgan, or us? You decide.

* In Morgan's defence, he does appear to possess the ability to send himself up (unlike some other celebrity fans): a substantial part of the column we read consisted of amusingly abusive emails he'd been sent by agitated readers.

Post-match interviews

It's not the banal questions or the clichéd response. It's not even the corporate logo-a-thon that forms the eye-dazzling backdrop to said interview. And, surprisingly, it's not even Garth Crooks. No, what really does our heads in during the post-match interview is the annoying sideways glance the player *always* does about a minute and a half in. Don't believe us? Just sit back, watch and wait.

Something really f*****g riveting must be happening just off camera. Surely, there's a finite number of times you can be lured into sneaking a peek at the moonie being pulled from a half-opened dressing room door, or the hilarious 'rabbit ears' sign a teammate is making behind the soundman's back?

This shifty look off camera reminds us that professional footballers are really just naughty little schoolboys desperate to play along with their mates' juvenile antics. The only difference is that the glance and barely suppressed smirk aren't carried out during a ticking off by the headteacher, they are done on Gabriel Clarke's watch, and in front of a comatose TV audience of thousands.

Renegade linesmen

There is one thing guaranteed to improve results in park football. Not a ringer who once had a trial at Southend. Not a fitness coach. Not even a box of expensive isotonic drinks. You will never guess, but you will understand: it is a dodgy linesman. Sorry, referee's assistant. Call them what you like, it is essential to have a lino who knows when to put the flag up – and we don't mean when a player is offside.

In Sunday football it is often better to start with ten players and still proffer someone to run the line for you. The dodgy lino's rationale goes something like this: irrespective of whether the player is offside, if he looks likely to score, stick the effin' flag up. The referee can always over-rule the linesman, but everyone knows the whole system is likely to break down if he does this too often. Thus, the corrupt linesman can stick his flag up, safe in the knowledge that he'll save his side a goal or two.

You have to have a thick skin to carry this off, because the abuse received is monstrous. The best of the worst linos will not respond. He will just stand there, resolutely with the flag up, oblivious to the complete breakdown in law and order that is going on around him. Yet this complete lack of emotion only fans the flames, as opposition players become increasingly irate. Maybe this is the plan, as the more wound up the opposing team becomes the less they concentrate on the game in hand.

The more confident linesman will also pull players up for foul throws. At amateur level a high proportion of throw-ins are fouls, but they are rarely penalised unless ludicrously obvious. The smarter bent linesman will – when their team is under pressure from a long-throw specialist – flag for a foul throw to help their team. As the ref is invariably following the flight of the ball, he is highly unlikely to overturn this decision.

This combination of flagging anything that moves and breaking up the flow of the game by awarding foul throws is worth at least 20 points a season. In Sunday football, having someone who will run the line is almost as vital as having someone who will wash the kit.

There is, however, a danger that things can go wrong – badly wrong. Every now and again a linesman goes AWOL, a bit like Colonel Kurtz in *Apocalypse Now*. This renegade linesman is usually a disgruntled substitute, coerced into running the line by his manager. Pissed off at weeks of being a sub week after week, running the line is the final straw. The renegade linesman turns on his teammates and refuses to flag for ANYTHING. Before they know quite what's hit them, the lino's own team find themselves 3-0 down as the result of three blatantly offside goals. For the dog-walking Sunday morning neutral there's nothing more exhilarating than watching this carnage unfold.

The language is coarse, and threats of violence are commonplace. Unlike the more studied 'dodgy' lino, the renegade is an active participant in the abuse, trading insults with *his* teammates. This sort of betrayal is what Sunday football is all about. Old scores are settled, years of pent-up frustration released. Then, as soon as the final whistle blows, the renegade linesman disappears into the jungle never to be seen again. Worry not though, it is usually nothing to do with a personal journey into the heart of darkness, and everything to do with a new job in Basingstoke.

Oh, 'The Horror, The Horror...' of being a Sunday morning linesman.

Rory Delap™

We were just wondering – has Rory Delap really gone to the bother of trademarking his 'trademark' long throw? And if so, is Alan Green legally obliged to refer to it as the 'Rory Delap long throw™' in any future broadcast?

It's not just the trade-marking issue either. There's all the fuss and bother surrounding the throw itself. This might come as a bit of a shock to mollycoddled Premier League bosses – but Delap isn't actually doing anything wrong. He's not even broken the Geneva Convention (a mandatory yellow card offence, according to the FIFA website). No, it's perfectly legal. With all the furore you'd think he was lobbing a uranium-enriched warhead into the penalty area, not a scruffy old size 5 football.

Sure, it's not pretty, but exactly how else are teams like Stoke expected to compete at the top table? They operate on a fraction of the big-boys' budget with a squad half the size. Who can really blame them for repeatedly trundling out their own 6-foot weapon of mass destruction. Of Stoke's first 13 goals in the 2008/09 Premier League campaign, seven were credited as Delap assists. That's a pretty good return. Let's hope Rory doesn't have to queue too long at the Patent Office; he's needed in the Potteries.

Rugby players or footballers: who's the hardest?

You don't need to be a genius to work out our stance on rugby, which makes this particular entry something of a foregone conclusion. But, in the spirit of the history's greatest show trials, we will endeavour to deliver our verdict in the most 'impartial' fashion possible...

We like football and we like to keep the company of fellow football fans, but every now and again we have to attend social functions dominated by 'the rugby lot'. Pretty, it ain't. Squashed noses and cauliflower ears proliferate to such an extent that should Steve Bruce saunter unannounced into the room, he'd be considered something of 'a looker'.

Then they open their mouths and it's like a 'Tim nice but dim' convention, with each rugby player trying to outdo the other with their cheery public school plumminess. Sure, rugby players are far more eloquent in post-match interviews than their football counterparts, but that's what a £16,000-a-year private education does for you. The only time the accent slips is when they embark on one of their oh-so-hilarious sing-songs about 'balls hanging low, dangling to and fro'. How can that humourless ditty compare to the terrace Tchaikovsky who thought up 'You're shit and you know you are'? It can't.

Thus far we've concluded that footballers are better looking, funnier and less affected due to the lack of an expensive education, but this doesn't help us decide who is hardest – rugby players or footballers? It is the question that always crops up when we are eventually 'outed' as football fans at one of these rugby gatherings. The conversation usually goes something like this:

Impossibly cheery rugby-type: 'Do you play then?'

One of us: 'What, rugby? Err, no, not since school. I'm more of a footballer myself.'

Rugby-type (losing some of his cheery demeanour): 'Football, eh? Never liked it. Can't stand all that rolling around on the floor as if you've been shot. You want to try a real man's sport. You footballers wouldn't last five minutes in a scrum.'

Us (thinking to ourselves): 'I wouldn't go within a five-mile radius of your 'effing scrum mate; you grabbing my nuts and twisting them 360 degrees isn't my idea of fun.'

Us (actually responding): 'Yes, well perhaps I should give it a go, never too late to learn, eh?'

Rugby-type: 'That's the spirit, we'll make a decent hooker out of you yet.'

Us: 'Great.'

Us (secretly thinking): 'Hooker? Me? I'd love to go straight through you with a Vinny Jones style two-footed tackle.'

As you can see, we've had plenty of opportunities to chew the cud on this one, and now it is time to deliver our verdict.

Pound for pound there's no contest: even your average prop-forward is going to make Richard Dunne or Danny Shittu look a little lightweight, but as our wives keep telling us, size isn't everything.

Both rugby and football are full-blooded contact sports and although the football authorities are doing their best to tone down the physical aspect of the game, there's still plenty of hard men knocking about. The same is true of rugby; it is only in recent years that biting and gouging have been outlawed from the not-so-beautiful game. If it were down to the amount of violence allowed on the field of play, rugby would win hands down. But that doesn't make them any harder – rugby players just get away with more. Both rugby and football enjoy their fair share of punch-ups, but when they happen in football they are all over the back pages of the papers for days on end. In rugby, the same punch-up is usually put down to 'high spirits' or a 'competitive edge'.

It's true that there is far too much play-acting in football. The sight of Cristiano Ronaldo rolling around on the floor clutching a knee after a defender came within two yards of him is one of the most depressing sights in football. The likelihood is that players of Ronaldo's ilk are more likely to get injured performing the pathetic, theatrical dives than they are from the challenge itself. Their play-acting doesn't do football any favours; it is one of the few areas where rugby comes out on top – and that's saying something!

To reach a meaningful conclusion on this debate we need to strip things down to basics. Growing up in the 1970s and '80s the distinction was simple: the posh kids played rugby; the nutters played football. We were left in no doubt who was hardest. It came down to who you'd cross the street to avoid – and that was *always* the football psycho. Every school team had three or four of them: the most outrageously talented players on the pitch were also the most mentally unhinged. Think back to your childhood. Think back to the best player on your team; he was also the toughest kid in school.

Maybe it's a class thing. The toughest kids were always the working-class ones and they were *always* the best at football. But we're not just talking kids' football. Who would you rather have on your side in a scrap? Dave Mackay, Vinny Jones, Graeme Souness or Bill Beaumont? Case closed. It really is as simple as that.

The thrust of this isn't that we (the authors) think we're tougher than our rugby-playing counterparts. True, we both love a tackle as much as the next crap Sunday footballer, but we are also the first to hide behind our big centre-half should things get a bit punchy. This is not an exercise in middle-aged machismo; we are simply doing our bit to re-dress the popular misconception that footballers are soft. We've both done our time in Sunday League and, believe us, there is nothing more scary than a heavily tattooed man, still drunk from the previous night's excesses, offering you the chance to 'sort things out' in the car park after the game. Even our five-a-side league gets a bit hairy at times. What these rugby-types need to consider is that us footballers have to deal with a high proportion of the nation's psychopaths on a weekly basis.

On a more positive note, we have a very effective early warning system in use at five-a-side; if an opponent has a club crest tattooed on his calf and is wearing builders' boots, under no circumstances should you attempt to tackle him (because he *will* kill you).

So, for all the rugby fraternity's protestations, football is much harder. It's not about surviving being stamped on as the scrum collapses or having your nuts bitten by some bloke in the second row. It's about getting out of the car park with your face intact – living to play another day.

Quite simply, it boils down to: posh kids versus nutters; prep school versus borstal. It's football – no contest.*

* Obviously, we are lily-livered cowards, so we'd be grateful if you'd keep this one under your hat. The last thing we want is to be trapped in a room full of big, burly rugby fellas and have one of them pipe up, 'I say, aren't you one of the chaps who called all rugby players big, ugly, humourless dullards?' Who's the toughest now, eh?

Rush, Stick or Scramble

The 1970s and '80s were littered with unlikely triumvirates: the airways were soothed by the timeless folk-harmonies of Peter, Paul, and Mary; on kids' telly Rod, Jane and Freddy had their hands full keeping Zippy, George and Bungle in check on ITV's seminal *Rainbow*; while over on BBC, *Mary, Mungo and Midge* was the first children's programme to tackle the problems of urban living head-on (albeit in animated form) with Mary, her dog Mungo and pet mouse Midge routinely spending entire episodes being trapped in the lift of their high-rise tower block.

But, while the above were important cultural reference points for any youngster growing up in that era, none had quite the same day-to-day impact as *Rush, Stick and Scramble*.

Before any playground football match could get under-way, the issue of 'Rush, Stick or Scramble' had to be resolved – it was as integral to a break-time kickabout as the ball itself. But for those of you who were either home educated (weirdos) or went to prep school (toffs) let us explain the basic premise behind Rush, Stick or Scramble.

In the 1970s playground football stood alone, outside FIFA's remit. As such, rules were few and games were rough. Free kicks were unheard of, and penalties only ever used to settle a tied game at the end of break (and only then as a bit of a change from 'next goal wins').

When setting up a game at break or lunch, speed was of the essence: at morning break you might only have ten or 15 minutes of football, so there was no hanging about. Sides were often picked during the preceding lesson, with any stragglers being dished out accordingly. Sometimes the sides were fair, with the best players being kept apart and the crap kids being divvied out to either team. Other times, you'd get whole year groups playing against each other in a free-for-all battle for bragging rights.

If the game had few rules, it had even fewer positions. Essentially you either played up front or you went in goal. And this is where 'Rush, Stick or Scramble' kicks in. Once the teams were picked, you had to decide what to do about keepers. Occasionally, you found a kid who was genuinely willing to go in nets, but most of the time tact, diplomacy, bribery or plain physical violence were deployed in picking a goalie. Yet finding a willing occupant was only part of the problem. The type of goalkeeping still had to be decided.

'Rush' goalie was usually deployed if the match was light on players, or the sides were unbalanced. 'Rush' essentially meant that the nominated keeper could play out on the pitch as well. With Jimmy Glass still a twinkle in his father's eye, the 'rush' goalie would regularly pop up at the other end of the pitch and knock in the winning goal. With hindsight – and a marginally better grasp of the rules of football – we realise that *all* goalies are 'rush' goalies; there is no restriction on keepers coming out of their area.

But as 11-year-olds the distinction between 'rush' and 'stick' was important. Obviously, if you were a 'stick' goalie, you were bound to remain in close proximity to the piles of jumpers that formed your goal. Again, there were no area markings in playground football, so the whole notion of being a 'stick' goalie now seems rather arbitrary ('stuck' to what exactly?). The final option was perhaps the most exciting and ground-breaking: 'scramble' goalie essentially meant *anyone* could go in goal.

It was disorganised chaos. Whoever was nearest the goal could legitimately use his hands to save the ball. It wasn't popular amongst the purists, but it added to the wild-west feel of playground matches. It also added to the disputes, as three or four players on the goal-line would frantically try and scramble the ball clear with their hands – the resulting penalty appeals either fell on deaf ears or facilitated an almighty scrap.

Of course, none of this was set in stone. Matches would oscillate between 'rush,' 'stick' and 'scramble' in the course of a morning break. Much would depend on how the game was going. If one team was tonking the other, the winning team would have their keeper 'stuck' while the team chasing the game would be allowed 'rush' keeper. 'Scramble' would often be employed when the poor sods in goal had had enough of the inevitable abuse and gone to seek refuge with the geeky kids discussing the previous night's *Think of a Number*.

We often wonder if 'Rush, Stick and Scramble' are still alive and well in the nation's playgrounds. We sometimes also think that 'proper' football could benefit from the unpredictability of scramble keepers. For years, 'Rush, Stick or Scramble' has existed outside of FIFA's jurisdiction; perhaps now it is time for Sepp to get it added to the statute books – it might just liven things up.

Signature haircuts

There's been a lot of talk about footballers' hair. Maybe too much talk.

Top Ten lists of crap haircuts litter the internet; there's been books and telly programmes – all legally obliged to feature: Kevin Keegan's bubble perm; Chris Waddle's mullet; Jason Lee's pineapple; Roberto Baggio's divine ponytail; and the Bobby Charlton/Ralph Coates comb-over (the last two always seemed a tad harsh as they had more to do with genetics than styling *per se*).

Anyway, our beef is this – an extravagant barnet should be for life, not just for Christmas.

If legend is to be believed, half of Merseyside had a bubble perm in the early 1980s: Souness, McDermott and Phils, Neal and Thompson, all went with a tight perm at some point during their Anfield careers. And half our school turned up with the Chrissy Waddle perma-mullet in 1986. But who's wearing one now? It's easy to follow the crowd; it's a lot harder to strike out on your own and maintain your signature haircut when it's no longer fashionable.

Every time we see Graeme Souness on the telly, we think how much better it would be if he were still sporting his perm-and-tash combo. Same goes for Chris Waddle. And Keegan shouldn't be allowed back into football management until he's gone back to the perm – we'd bloody love it if that happened.

Some players transcend their haircuts; others succumb. We think the latter is the more dignified option. After all, surely Chris Waddle would prefer to be remembered for his dodgy hair than for blasting a penalty high over the bar in a World Cup semi-final? So, we salute the men prepared to stand by their hair. Unfortunately, we've only found a couple.

Carlos Valderrama's orange-tinged frizz is the same today as it was during USA '94, when he strutted around the Rose

Bowl like a strawberry-blonde Tom Baker during a particularly sweaty episode of *Dr Who*. Even the statue of Valderrama erected at the Eduardo Santos stadium in his hometown of Santa Marta is topped with an enormous metallic-orange frizz. Carlos is clearly a man who has learned to embrace his haircut – there'll be no Francis Rossi-style shearing for him.

The only other football legend who hasn't abandoned his trademark hairdo is Alan Biley. The much-travelled striker turned out for Cambridge United, Derby County, Everton, Stoke City, Portsmouth and Brighton and is remembered as much for his hair as his goals. Biley was a cult legend at Fratton Park, where he scored 51 goals in 101 appearances, an achievement made even more remarkable by the fact that he appeared to be borrowing Rod Stewart's hair.

Since hanging up his boots, Biley has had a successful career in non-league management – and this is where we confirmed his dedication to his barnet. We were having a half-time drink in the bar at Brackley Town's St James Park when Alan Biley strode in. He didn't look a day older than we remember him in his Pompey pomp and he had *exactly* the same hair! Least, we're pretty sure it was him; if it wasn't, then this fella could've made a good career out of being a looky-likey.

Assuming it was Biley – and we're fairly confident as he's a regular on the local non-league scene and had links with Brackley's opponents that day, Corby Town – then our admiration knows no bounds. Unlike Messrs Waddle and Keegan, Biley has stayed true to his roots and remained loyal to his signature hair – hats off to you, Alan.

Sketchy past

We have accumulated plenty of cheap plastic trophies during our careers in the musty catacombs below the pyramids of real football, but we have yet to win a sketch of ourselves, and a mysterious glass 'memento'. (What was this memento exactly? We doubt we'll ever know.) Yet a number of top professionals managed to secure such an honour by playing well – for a month – in the 1980s.

The *Daily Mirror* bestowed this honour to the player they believed had played the best during the previous calendar month. Looking back, we suspect the winner was the only player that agreed to accept the award. Agents would hardly be rubbing their hands waiting for the cut of this particular achievement, even if this was the dark, desperate '80s when financial rewards were few and column inches at a premium.

Can you imagine players like Ronaldo or Bellamy turning up to receive a glass memento and a sketch of themselves that wasn't even in colour? There would be more likelihood of Roy Race pitching up in cardboard cut-out form.

A photo of the player receiving the award from a *Daily Mirror* representative usually accompanied a short interview. 'Just how was that 40-yard volley scored, Brian?' Oddly, the award didn't ever go to a player who had played well, but had *not* featured on the telly. A couple of cameos on *Sportsnight* was usually enough to secure the prize.

Leafing through the *Mirror* over breakfast, it was always a pleasant shock to meet the next recipient, because we often forgot that the award existed at all. You would turn the page and there was the winner – no fuss, bother or protracted phone vote. There never seemed to be any set day or date that it was handed out, either. The feature would also appear and then stop without warning in mid-season, or so it seemed.

We would love to think that these sketches are hanging in pride of place in various ex-pros' houses or pubs. More likely they were lost or given away. It would be wonderful to see one turn up on *Antiques Roadshow* or *Cash In The Attic*. Sketches of '80s journeymen would be priceless, but what value would Jennie Bond place on that mysterious glass 'memento'?

Skins

Skins. No, not the amphetamine-fuelled E4 yoof shag-a-thon that would have Mary Whitehouse spinning in her grave (and that makes us feel *very* old). Not even a hot summer's afternoon down the rec, with one side in shirts and the other stripped to the waist.

No, we are taking about *Skins* (also referred to as 'second-skins', 'base layers' or even 'body armour'), the ridiculous layer of lycra that every professional footballer has taken to wearing under their shirts. Apparently, they regulate body temperature, wick moisture and guarantee you 20 goals a season. Shame they also make you look like a twat. The bizarre FIFA ruling that they have to match the colour of your shirt doesn't help much. Nor does the stupid roll-neck collar.

Are today's footballers really too young to remember the short-lived cycling-shorts boom of the early 1990s? Same shit idea: skin-tight lycra sold as a technological break-through. For about three weeks in 1991, cycling shorts were heralded as *the* cure for hamstring injuries. Yep, slip into a pair of these miracle shorts and you could kiss goodbye to six weeks out injured with a muscle pull. And they made your arse look smaller. Control pants for footballers – bonus.

Hopefully, the skins phenomenon will be similarly short and sweet. It should be.

Slaves to the rhythm

Every time we sit down to write something about the Cristiano Ronaldo/Sepp Blatter slavery furore we get stuck. We just can't shake that image of Jabba the Hut and Princess Leia in *The Return of the Jedi*.

Not that it matters, because Sepp is denying everything, 'I have never said that Ronaldo is a slave,' he said, before neglecting to add, 'I bet he looks good in a bikini and chains, mind.'

Snatch of the Day

It's not what you think. We know the internet has brought pornography to the masses, but we are not interested in any of that.

The 'snatch' in question involved a classic public information film from the mid-1970s. Warning of the dangers of pick pockets, an impossibly cheery man in a sheepskin coat (à la Motty) and a wide-boy pundit provide the chilling voiceover to a snatch carried out in broad daylight in Piccadilly Circus. As kids, it all seemed a bit sinister and, for a while, left us shaking with fear every time our mums suggested a day trip to London.

What really freaked us out about *Snatch of the Day* was the extended football metaphor. The advert began with a generic sports programme-type jingle – like the bastard son of *The Big Match* and *Midweek Sports Special* music, belted out on a primitive keyboard. The graphics, overlaid on an impressive set of floodlights, echoed those of *Match of the Day*. Then, to round things off, these acts of petty crime were all voiced with a football-style commentary, and all done without a hint of irony. This was the 1970s personified.

Eventually, we overcame our fears, and learned to love this public information film – we'd even jump about the room when it came on. Look it up on the internet and see for yourself. It was an advert that all fans could identify with. Only Ian Rush's Accrington Stanley milk advert or John Barnes' effort for Lucozade Sport could rival it in football fans' affection.

How could anyone possibly dispute the greatness of an advert that closes with the following exchange?

Commentator: 'Tell me, where is it impossible to snatch?'
Wide-boy pundit: 'A nudist colony.'

Of course, there was a serious message behind it all, and we suggest it is now reprised to highlight the pickpocketing of the modern game by greedy investors looking for celebrity, fame and short-term gain. Militant filmmakers, get to it.

Snood not to

We've already done gloves, turtle-neck sweaters and men-in-tights, and we thought it couldn't get any worse, but it did.

On 9th December 2007 at White Hart Lane, football haute couture hit an all-time low. It was a fashion faux-pas too far. In the 53rd minute Manchester City's Roland Bianchi came off the bench and entered the field of play wearing a snood. Yes, that's right: a snood – an item of clothing last seen on *Ski Sunday* in 1985 being worn by Franz Klammer.

For the uninitiated, a snood (and this is the Wikipedia definition) 'is a tubular neck warmer that can be worn either pulled down around the neck like a scarf or up over the hair like a hood'. Bianchi chose the former – it didn't stop him looking any less of an idiot.

Football is an athletic activity – if you are cold, try running about a bit more. What was Bianchi thinking? He looked ridiculous. The only saving grace was that it turned out to be home-made. He'd simply cut the collar off an old jumper, probably the one George Michael was wearing in the video for *Last Christmas*. So, at least, Roland hadn't paid a fortune to some Milan fashionista for this abomination. And, even better, the look never caught on – the Premier League has remained snood-free ever since.

Spin doctors

If not able to play football, supporters everywhere search for football-related games. Subbuteo ruled the roost in the 1970s, but these days computer simulation or manager games are popular options. Yet there was one other game that found its way into everyone's household at one time or another – and that was table football.

With televised matches a rarity, table football was an excellent way to utilise your football fanaticism and energy. No football on the box? Play table football. Bad weather? Play table football. It was a great competitive football diversion when nothing else was on offer.

Two teams of 11 men with metal rods through their backs may be every woman's dream, but this wasn't torture night at the WI – it was table football. Luckily, unlike Subbuteo or computer games, women did not need to know the rules: just twist the knob and get the ball in the hole at either end – if only everything in life was that simple. The advantage of it being so easy was that you could convince anyone to play: Aunty Beryl; your next-door neighbour; the Avon lady – anyone who turned up at your house could be convinced to give table football a try. This was important, as it was not a game that could be played by one person. Ideally, table football needs four players, especially if played by children with small wingspans.

The early tables on offer were expensive, but soon '80s consumerism drove the prices down and it became a staple Christmas present. And like all great Christmas gifts the game left you with blisters and various other aches and pains – think Crossfire, Twister or the Mr Frosty ice drink maker. Setting up the game during the festive period could be problematic: if you did not have a place for a table with legs, then no problem, don't bother attaching the legs, just plonk it on the dining table, but at Christmas the dining room was in high demand, leading to direct confrontation with your mum, as she battled to lay the table for dinner.

In table football, the classic layout was, and is: one goalie, two defenders, five midfielders and three strikers. It is believed that this was how David Moyes formulated his plan to have a team stuffed full of midfielders. Rumours persist that he disembowelled two of his strikers and relocated them on the midfield rod, but we've uncovered no firm evidence. The pitch itself could be glass-topped or open plan. Glass-topped tables encouraged drinks to be placed on them, with the obvious peril of liquid spilling everywhere as the excitement intensified. Open-topped tables made it easier for cheats to move the ball with their hands, and were apparently very popular in Argentina.

As for the game itself, two tactics quickly evolved. The first was the frenzied attacking of the ball with no thought of where it was going. However, once some basic skills had been acquired a slower-paced tactical game emerged where thought was given to where and to whom the ball was played.

But one great tactical controversy has plagued the game throughout its history – spinning. The obvious tactic when the ball is ricocheting around is to generate power by spinning your players around at high speed, then letting go of the handle. The ball flies around the table at speeds approaching Mach One and, if caught just right, soon flashes past the goalkeeper and into the net. The only skill needed is the ability to spin the rod at high speed. Spin was the favoured tactic of younger siblings and Alistair Campbell. As participants grew older there was generally an agreement before play commenced that spinning was not allowed – a table football pre-nuptial, if you like.

When we played as youngsters, despite these treatises, there were frequent attempts to get away with mini-spins without being noticed. Novices to the game or less skillful players used this tactic often and without remorse. The issue of spinning caused countless games to be abandoned as competitors gave up table football, preferring instead to wrestle each other to the ground and bludgeon each other around the head with stray pieces of Meccano.

A whole generation of retro-players were up in arms over an episode of *Friends* involving a 'fussball table'. Monica beat Chandler and Joey single-handed and finished by scoring a goal with a vicious spin shot. There is no way that would have been allowed in any of our games. Younger siblings can get away with it – adults should know better.

Another problem that invaded the sport of table football was a sloping pitch. This occurred due to warped pitches, or different length table legs. It affected the smooth running of the ball, causing it to get stuck in places where the players could not reach it. Unauthorised tilting of the table was often the only way to move the ball unless hands were used. However, unless agreed by both parties, it was deemed as cheating.

Football tables used to be found in pubs, clubs and arcades all over the country, but these are becoming rare. Some can occasionally be found in office or factory staff rooms. Table football continues to flourish around the world (especially in Germany and Latin America), but back in Blighty the football table has been reduced to an executive plaything: trendy magazines feature expensive tables finished in mahogany or teak – you can even have teams individually hand crafted. Football tables have become status symbols for bored bankers, rather than the toy we played with for hours as children. The simplicity and gameplay of the football table ensures it will remain part of British culture, but it will never be as well loved as it was when we were kids – and no amount of spin from these executive plaything manufacturers can convince us otherwise. £999 for table football? Ours cost a tenner from Woolies.

Stinging Nettles

It was an unlikely marriage, but it happened. Keegan might've been the face (and chest hair) of Brut, but the man who replaced him as the idol of the Kop, Kenny Dalglish, *was* the '80s face of Jersey. What? You thought that was Bergerac?

Even now we can't make sense of it. Dalglish was about as Scottish as they come. We remember watching him interviewed by Motty on *Football Focus*, and we couldn't understand a bloody word. What was he doing advertising the Channel Islands? It was the '80s we suppose, a time when even a top-flight footballer had to do a spot of moonlighting to make ends meet. But Jersey? Home of cows, potatoes and a favoured bolt-hole for those looking to, err, 'park' their offshore investments.

It made no sense. Had the Jersey Tourist Board picked Dalglish out at random? Or had King Kenny enjoyed a holiday on the island so much that he wanted to spread the gospel?

Perhaps Kenny had wanted to promote the Hebrides, but found Hot-Shot Hamish had already secured the gig? And when Nigel Mansell bagged the Isle of Man, Kenny thought he'd better act fast. We'll never know for sure, but one thing is for certain: the real '80s face of Jersey, John Nettles, was left spitting feathers.

Streakers

We blame reality TV. Back in the 1970s and '80s, if you wanted fame and tabloid notoriety, you didn't have to mope around the *Big Brother* house for ten weeks with a camera trained on your every move. No, all you had to do was get your knockers out at a major sporting event.

Erica Rowe and Sheila Nicholls became celebrities in their own right, by simply whipping off their clothes and legging it across a pitch. And, of course, their pioneer spirit prompted a host of copycat incidents at football grounds all over Britain. But it didn't last. TV companies wised up and refused to give the streakers any airtime. Depriving them of television exposure sorted out the celebrity wannabes from those who just like getting naked in public – and the result was a drastic reduction in streaking at sporting events.

It was a shame, as a good streak could enliven the dullest of fixtures. As lads going to football in the '70s it brought a touch of erotica to the football calendar. But witnessing a streak wasn't just some excuse to ogle naked women – it was a genuine cultural phenomenon. Did the decade really produce anything funnier than the sight of a naked bloke being escorted around the edge of the pitch with a policeman's helmet covering his, err, helmet? Witnessing a streaker at the football was a 1970s right of passage right up there with busting your nads on the crossbar of your Raleigh Chopper. Ouch.

Sub standards

The behaviour of substitutes is in decline. Barely a weekend goes by without subs falling asleep, pulling faces and generally behaving like naughty 12-year-olds on a school trip. We put it down to the increased numbers allowed in league and European games.

When we were growing up there was only ever one sub, and they knew exactly where they stood (or sat). They had to be primed and ready to play at all times in case of injuries, sendings off or tactical responses. There was no sleeping for the single sub. He was regularly seen dancing up and down the touchline, or barking encouragement to the rest of the team.

The antics of modern-day substitutes hardly reinforces the professional image of the game. Many listen to MP3 players wrapped up in bench jackets, hats, scarves and gloves. Some even drape those tartan picnic blankets – last seen in the back of your Nan's Ford Zephyr – over their legs in an attempt to keep warm. Gone are the wooden benches of old, replaced instead by futuristic car seats in luxurious leather, embossed with the club crest – given such creature comforts, is it any wonder the modern sub drifts off to sleep?

Listening to music, sharing a joke, even texting friends or relatives appears to be the prime objective for today's peripheral squad members. As passionate fans we want to see them involved and interacting in the game. We see Fergie shouting and jumping up and down on the touchline when a goal is scored or a bad decision made. If we were substitutes, we would be there alongside him, chivvying along our teammates out on the pitch. Gary Neville may not have many fans, but at least we know he cares. Whether Red Nev is playing or on the bench he makes sure he gets involved.

The players are, we hope, disappointed not to be in the starting line-up and desperate to be out on the pitch. We would expect them to be badgering the manager incessantly for a chance to come on, much like Donkey asking Shrek, 'Are we there yet?' every five minutes on the journey to the Kingdom of Far, Far Away.

This may not endear the player to a manager focusing on the game, but at least he would know the player cared. The other option would be to warm up constantly with great enthusiasm. This has to be better than just sleeping through a game?

There are a number of options available to clubs to sort out the substitutes' behaviour. The first is to make them less comfortable. No more leather seats; just a wooden bench so they cannot relax too much. Ban phones, MP3 players and all other electronic gizmos. Then throw away the heavy-duty padded bench jackets and go back to a tracksuit top like the old players used to wear. That way, the only option for keeping warm is to move about. Also, make sure the bench is not under cover, so that the players are exposed to the elements like their teammates. This might not quite be in line with the top medical advice, but it never did us any harm.

Another option is to keep the existing seats, but link them up to an electric shock machine. Each week a fan could be put in charge of monitoring the substitutes' behaviour. When they become too comfortable the fan could send an electric shock to liven them up. Three blasts and the player is not allowed to participate in the match – no win bonus or appearance money, and perhaps even a fine. Put these measures in place and players would be out warming up pretty sharpish, ensuring they were focused on the game. Clubs unable to afford a sophisticated system like this could provide the monitoring fan with a crate of rotten fruit to throw at the offenders – cheaper but equally effective.

Substituted players should not be able to walk off the pitch directly to the changing rooms, either. They should be made to sit and watch the rest of the match, showing solidarity with their teammates. This is especially important if the team are losing as a result of that player's lacklustre efforts. We don't care it they are injured. Stick some ice or a bandage on it, and sit there with everyone else. Too often, underperforming players are allowed the luxury of a shower or bath by themselves. We then see them reappear in their own clothes ready for a night on the town. If you are substituted you should not be happy, whatever the reason. We want to see players throwing and kicking things when they come off, because that is what we do. Seeing your number held up on the electronic board shouldn't be a relief, it should trigger a childish temper-tantrum – crates of isotonic drinks should be sent flying and shirts should be flung in the direction of the manager.

These rules would bring players closer to the fans and improve the spectacle of the game. The shirkers would know exactly where they stood. We do not need players happy to pick up their wages and sit on the substitutes' bench. We need to see they care, not just be told that they do by a sanctimonious agent. Actions speak louder than words. For the good of the game, football can no longer tolerate this sub-standard behaviour.

Terrace vernacular

We don't watch that much football on the telly, but occasionally we'll sit down with a glass of warm milk and some Rich Tea biscuits and watch a bit of ITV's Champions League Tuesday.

As much as it pains us to say it, sometimes both the football and the coverage can be quite good. We're even slowly warming to the Clive Tyldesley/David Pleat double act, mostly because – try as we might – we just can't seem to synch the Radio 5 Live commentary with the action on the screen.

Anyway, there's one thing that really gets to us with the commentary – and no, it's not the regular references to 'that night in Barcelona'; Uncle Clive is merely teasing us with that one – it is the duo's constant need to talk about 'the fans on the terraces'. David and Clive*, look around you: what effin' terraces? It's one of the requirements of the bloody Champions League not to have terraces.

In fact, next time you rock up at a European tie in Germany, get to the ground really early and you might witness the terracing behind the goals being converted to seating ready for your match. In European competition, as in the top two tiers of English football, fans on the terraces are as mythical as the man on the Clapham omnibus.

So, please stop referring to the terraces. Why not experiment a little? How about, 'the hardworking fan who has forked out 110 Euros to sit in a crappy plastic bucket seat behind the goal', or 'the corporate freeloader who is sitting in the posh seats just in front of the pressbox, chatting to his client and paying zero attention to the match'.

Most real fans were priced out of European football years ago and are probably at home watching on the telly – just bear that in mind. Thanks.

*We suspect that it's not just Clive and David who are guilty of this particular faux pas, so apologies for singling them out in such a brutal way, but we really don't get to watch much football on TV.

The People versus Michel Platini

It seems everyone has got it in for St Michel. Well, when we say *everyone* we mean the highly influential British press. And although most members of the Fourth Estate are only to eager too have a pop at Platini, we actually have one particular journalist in mind – Martin Samuel.

It is a clash of football's heavyweights. One is a highly influential middle-aged man, with a mop of browny-black hair and a slight paunch. The other is Michel Platini. These men have at loggerheads for the past couple of years, although to be fair to Michel, he probably hasn't noticed. But Martin Samuel just refuses to let it lie.

According to his biography on *The Times* website, Samuel is a seven times winner of the Sports Writer of the Year award and the most successful sports journalist of his generation. We're not too sure about that last bit as we were raised on a diet of Harry Harris and the *Daily Mirror*. But we can't dispute the awards or the ringing endorsement from the judges who heralded Samuel's 'trenchant, fearless views, combined with wit and irony and the memorably killer phrase'.

But for the glowing testimony of his Fleet Street peers, all we see is a one-man war being waged against UEFA president, Michel Platini. To wit, some headline articles from Martin's *Times* column: *Michel Platini in Champions League fantasy world* (22 October 2008); *English football at risk from French revolution* (19 November 2008); *Europe should say non to Platini's interference* (24 November 2008).

Poor old Platini. We're still not entirely sure what he's done to deserve this. We quite like the bloke. In fact, the thought of yet another all-English Champions League final has us jumping on the first ferry out of Dover, heading across La Manche and into Michel's loving, egalitarian arms. We must be seriously out of step with popular opinion, which, come to think of it, is why we don't have a column in a national newspaper.

Then, as we penned our first draft on this topic, Martin Samuel vanished from *The Times*. Further investigation revealed that he had been subject to a big money transfer to the *Daily Mail* (the *Media Guardian* reported a salary in excess of £400,000). We can only assume the normally inclusive *Mail* fancied joining in with a bit of healthy Platini-baiting. In fact, quite a journalistic 'dream-team' being assembled at the *Mail* – first Piers Morgan (*see* Pierless), then Martin Samuel.

But, although the articles continued, such as: *UEFA President Platini highlights the danger of showing your true colours* (25 February 2009) and *Our league is healthy when you look below Platini and his 'big four'* (5 May 2009), the vitriol directed at Monsieur Platini didn't have the same intensity. We couldn't quite work it out. Perhaps, with so many other things to worry about at Mail HQ – house prices, asylum seekers, the nanny state, inheritance tax, the EU, single parents, impotence, gay vicars, bird flu, swine flu, goat flu and (our personal favourite) Britain's out-of-control wheelie-bins – there just wasn't time to pick on Platini.

Anyhow, Martin Samuel and the *Daily Mail* seem like a match made in heaven. But it's left us wondering if there's a vacancy for a couple of outspoken columnists at *The Times?*

There's only 101 great goals

There are only 101 great goals. Anyone who suggests otherwise is lying. We know, because we have the video. Most of the country has the video. It has Bobby Charlton on the front and contains loads of goals – 101 to be precise. The great goals that the BBC recorded before 1987, that is. And chosen by the BBC. So, no arguments then. Find it, buy it and watch it. You will see 101 great goals. It does exactly what it says on the cover.

This video was a rite of passage for all football fans at the end of the '80s. We had never seen anything like it. Loads and loads of goals on one tape – great ones at that. Videos were new. We thought they were just for films. Suddenly this video arrived. Men and boys rejoiced. We had all seen the goals before on the Beeb. That familiarity made us agree that they were great. And because they were all on video we could watch them again and again and again.

Suddenly there was a surfeit of videos claiming to contain the greatest goals ever scored. Some didn't even claim they were great, just giving a number of goals and the league they came from. From an era where football was rationed and a low percentage of games were actually recorded, there were suddenly recordings and releases of everything. It was both brilliant and crap at the same time. The downside was simple: if you'd seen a goal that no one else had you could tell your mates how great it was without the fear that anyone would've actually seen it – video killed the playground brag (almost) overnight. On the plus side, you finally got to see your team's goals on one video.

The *101 Great Goals* video even seeped into popular culture: Danny Boyle's film adaptation of *Trainspotting* to be precise. Unbeknown to Tommy, his mate Renton had swapped a video of *101 Great Goals* with a homemade sex-tape of Tommy and his girlfriend. Renton then borrowed *101*

Great Goals. After a night out, Tommy's girlfriend wanted to watch their amateur video while shagging. He sticks the tape in the VCR only to see Archie Gemmill tucking away his famous goal against Holland at the 1978 World Cup. Tommy thinks he has returned *101 Great Goals* to the video rental shop and thinks all of Scotland has seen the tape. As a result, his relationship breaks up and he begins his descent into a drug-induced hell. But the most shocking part of all this is that Tommy didn't actually *own* the video!

If you ever find yourself in this scenario, you could do a lot worse than watch the rest of the video – the goals *are* outstanding. Plus, if your girlfriend wants to watch a home-made sex-tape, your life can't be all that bad.

Ticker-tape

A friend recently alerted us to a new product on the market – a personal confetti maker. It isn't pitched to bridesmaids and guests as the ultimate wedding accessory – far from it. The grim reality is that it is the next level up in personal document shredding. Don't want to run the risk of some deluded identify thief rummaging through your bins and trying to stick your credit card statements back together with Sellotape? Then turn your important documents into thousands of tiny bits of confetti and chuck them about at weddings. Good idea, heh?

All this talk of confetti got us thinking. We both realised we'd spent far too much of our youth ripping up telephone directories and *Yellow Pages* (for obvious, colour-related reasons, *Yellow Pages* became exceedingly difficult to source after mid-September in the Watford area) in a vain attempt to recreate the monsoon of ticker-tape we'd seen at Argentina '78. We'd often wondered why the Saturday mornings we'd spent shredding phone books (and not in a manly, *Guinness Book of Records* type way, either) had resulted in a dismal five-second flurry of ticker-tape.

We'd rashly assumed it was because our attempts at confetti production weren't backed by an all-powerful military junta. But now we know the truth – it's because the personal confetti maker hadn't been put before the panel on *Dragons' Den* yet.

Perhaps now we will see a revival of one of football's great 'lost arts' – a proper ticker-tape reception, the sort usually reserved for Superman, returning war veterans or World Cup Finals.

Once ticker-tape is back on the agenda, it will be time for bog-roll. Great swathes of it raining down on the penalty area, causing the goalkeeper to trip up every time he goes to take a goal kick and forcing men in fluorescent jackets to scurry about desperately trying to untangle the loo roll from the net when the ball is up the other end. And while we are on this revivalist trip, what about paper planes? Or inflatable haddock? If ticker-tape can return, so can they.

Tony Kempster RIP

In June 2009, football lost one of her most dedicated public servants – Tony Kempster. Anyone with more than a passing interest in non-league football will have heard of Tony, and more likely than not they will have come to rely on his excellent website: www.tonykempster.co.uk.

These days, we are so accustomed to zingy, all-action websites promising the earth but delivering very little, that we forget the primary purpose of the world wide web *should* be to impart information and share knowledge – something that is easily forgotten as you drown in a slew of tacky animated adverts. *Tony Kempster's English Football Site* stood as a much-needed antidote to all of this commercialised nonsense. Tony's site simply told you what you wanted to know – and fast.

Tony Kempster's website was a vital resource for non-league fans: it carried comprehensive fixtures, results, tables, crowds and mileages for every club down to Step 7 of the non-league pyramid, and went one level further – to Step 8 – for results and tables. This meant that, come Saturday evening, you could reliably check the website and find out the result of Welford Victoria v Wootton St George in Division One of the Northamptonshire Combination (a 3-2 win for Welford, 21/03/09, by the way).

Don't be fooled – this wasn't just a website for geeks, anoraks and stattos, this was a vital non-league resource for fans who care passionately about grassroots football.

It was about more than just results too: at the end of every season, non-league football goes through its own 'corridor of uncertainty' as clubs move between different leagues and divisions – often subject to meeting ground requirements or acceptance criteria. Tony's website tracked these changes and provided the definitive answer to this seasonal restructuring way ahead of anyone else.

This treasure-trove of information was brought to you with a minimum of fuss and an absence of superfluous graphics. In recent years, other websites began to delve into the (sometimes) murky world of non-league football. But none could match Tony Kempster's website for simplicity, accuracy and reliability.

In 2008, Tony's services to football were recognised by the Football Supporters' Federation (FSF), who honoured him with the Services to Supporters award. Malcolm Clarke, Chair of the FSF, said: 'Tony's website, produced on an entirely voluntary basis, has become an invaluable source of information for thousands of football fans each week. It carries a huge amount of information which no other site can match.'

Clarke also drew attention to the one vagary of *Tony Kempster's English Football Site*, the notable absence of top-flight fixtures (the Premier League wanted to charge Tony £9,000 so that he could publicise its fixtures on his site – he, quite rightly, refused): 'The only thing missing from his site are the fixtures of the Premier League and the Football League, because those organisations exercise their copyright to prevent Tony publishing them without paying an exorbitant fee. They should be ashamed of themselves.' Quite right too. However, the insatiable greed of football's moneymen should not cast a shadow over Tony's work. True fans know that the very soul of football rests safely with men and women of his ilk.

Tony kept working on his 'baby' even when gripped by ill-health; he left the site up-to-date with the final standings from the 2008/09 season. And, as we write, that's how it stands – a fitting memorial to one man's passion – a passion that brought joy to millions.

Too many singers spoil the Cup Final

FA Cup finals used to have a marching band. National anthems at international matches were played through a very old tannoy system linked up to what sounded like an original Dansette. Things were simple. Not that exciting, we grant you, but you knew exactly what to expect and when to expect it. Fans would sing the anthems, about two beats behind the band. That was tradition too.

Atmosphere should be fan generated. The rise of the televised match has meant that organisers demand a spectacle for the docile TV audience. At first the cameras would pan to members of the crowd singing. This gave a chance for fans to be recognised at home. Now the cameras focus on an already over-exposed celebrity singer.

Every occasion is celebrated by inviting someone to sing anthems or hymns. Classical artists like Katherine Jenkins are sucking the money out of football. Last year alone the amount spent on singers at football matches was larger than the national debt of Papua New Guinea. Probably. Some of the singers are not even singers. They are 'celebrities' who won a reality TV show, or someone who has 'always wanted to do it'.

Stop it now. It is a waste of time. If you have to do it, use local talent or at least someone who doesn't charge more than a season ticket price to perform. But we have a plan. We are a bit worried that Simon Cowell will nick our idea so we are putting it in print, so that everyone knows who thought of it first.

Crowd Idol is the chance for supporters across the nation to win the right to sing at the FA Cup final. Each club nominates a fan to sing for them. A knockout competition then runs in parallel with the real FA Cup. We want a passionate fan singing with, well, passion. Not necessarily the best singer, but someone who can portray the raw emotion of supporting their club.

It may be a rubbish idea, but at least we will be comforted by the knowledge that a pampered superstar has just lost their place at the Cup final.

Total recall

We know we are getting old. It takes us at least two days to recover from our Wednesday night kick-about – on Thursdays we can't get out of bed without dousing ourselves in Ralgex, and it is only by about four o'clock on a Friday afternoon that we can contemplate tackling the office stairs unaided.

But it's not our physical decline that frightens us (even in our pomp we were never in particularly great shape); it's the mental degeneration that gives us sleepless nights. Recently, we've found ourselves lying awake at night pondering stuff like, 'Who the f**k won the 2009 FA Cup?' You see, we can't remember anything about football after about 1986. Prior to that we're bloody geniuses.

This case of short-term memory loss has nothing to do with the supposed decline in stature of the FA Cup and everything to do with us. While the 2009 FA Cup final draws a blank, its 1979 counterpart has the memories flooding back. We can feel the sunshine, taste the sweat and hear Peter Jones' commentary as Alan Sunderland slides in a last-gasp winner at the far post: 'Brady for Arsenal, out to Rix, the ball floats high across the area, the shot comes in… it's there. 3-2. Alan Sunderland. I do not believe it, I swear I do not believe it.' It might've been dubbed the 'five-minute final' but it stayed with us forever.

World Cups are no better. The 2002 World Cup in Japan/Korea? Nothing but hazy images of David Beckham's broken metatarsal. The 1982 World Cup in Spain? Almost total recall. Brazil's manager? Easy – Telê Santana, the lollipop-sucking Kojak actor. Not sure how a TV detective got the Brazil job, but let's face it, a team containing Eder, Falcao, Socrates and Zico probably didn't need much in the way of man-management. We remember El Salvador's 10-1 tonking at the hands of Hungary. We remember Belgium's kit with the train tracks (made up of Admiral logos) that started on the shorts and went all the way up the shirts before disappearing under sweaty armpits. And we remember the official mascot, Naranjito – we loved that little orange fella.

These days – nothing. We were grateful to Zidane for nutting Materazzi at the 2006 World Cup as it helped us remember who was in the final, but don't ask us who won it.

It seems that no matter how hard we try or how long we spend trying those brain-training activities in the newspaper, we are stuck with the football memories of our youth. Everything else? It might've only happened yesterday, but we're buggered if we can remember it.

Maybe years from now, the football trivia of the early 21st century will come flooding back and, like Arnie, we'll have total recall. Here's hoping, eh?

Tree is the magic number

There are dwindling stocks of goalposts in our public parks as they are deemed a hazard by power-crazed Health & Safety types. Any surviving goalposts have often been vandalised to such an extent that they can't be used and present precisely the kind of danger that the Health & Safety mob keep going on about.

We are fed up with both the lack of posts and witnessing our parks and pitches being concreted over to make way for yet more starter homes. We need to rally behind the young-sters of today. We want them to be able to kick a ball about on grass.

We also stand shoulder-to-shoulder with the herbal tea-slurping environmentalists. We understand the need for parks to have trees, if only for dogs to pee up against. So, let us tell you about our scheme designed to keep all parties happy.

When any parks have new trees planted, please position them in twos about eight yards apart. If possible, plant an identical pair of trees, about 80 yards away. There you have it, green football pitches ready for all the family – and envi-ronmentally friendly too. Make some smaller tree goals and pitches for younger kids. Perhaps plant some small bushes for corner flags.

At the moment it is nigh on impossible to find a pair of trees the correct distance apart. We know, because we have looked.

What a legacy to leave the next generation of football superstars. It's what you might call grassroots soccer.

Tunnel vision

As kids, we waited all week for our next football fix. By 2.55pm on a Saturday afternoon the tension was unbearable. We stood on the terrace craning our necks, our eyes locked on a murky gap in the main stand. Sometimes, we'd see a club official (back then, a stately looking gentleman in a blazer; now, some fluorescent-jacketed health and safety goon) giving the signal; sometimes we'd just be swept along by the roar of better-positioned fans elsewhere in the ground. This was what we'd been waiting for – the players emerging from the tunnel and spilling out onto the pitch. It was a true 'butterflies in the stomach' moment.

Unfortunately, someone, somewhere in the higher echelons of football administration took the 'butterflies' thing literally. We are not sure exactly when it happened, but sometime in the late 1990s, the authorities decided it would be a great idea to stick giant, retractable, plastic caterpillars onto the end of tunnels everywhere. Fantastic.

The idea was to protect the players from those horrible little oiks who turn up at the ground every week: you know, the fans. Apparently, we'd been shouting stuff at them. Really nasty stuff like: '£120,000 a week? You've not even broken a sweat' and other things involving swearwords. Obviously, the FA had to act.

As a result, about 15 minutes before kick-off, the horrible plastic caterpillar is cranked up and out, providing our Premiership darlings safe passage to their place of work – the pitch. Of course, the plastic caterpillar doesn't just protect our pampered superstars from the hoi polloi, it is a fantastic branding opportunity. Yep, it's 24 feet of plastic festooned in logos – and it looks horrible. We want our players to emerge from the darkest recesses of our stadium and into the light. We don't want them to step out from under a glorified awning.

Then there's the whole protocol of the teams coming out of the tunnel together. It's rubbish. Half the fun was the pantomime booing of the away side as they took to the field, and the corresponding raising of the decibels when your side emerged. The teams coming out together is another pathetic attempt to sanitise the modern game.

To make it even worse, television cameras now have access to the tunnel. So, instead of waiting, with your stomach tied up in knots, for the teams to arrive, you can now watch them picking their noses and ruffling mascots' hair in the tunnel on the bloody giant screen. It's pathetic. It used to be an unwritten law of football that cameras were only allowed in the tunnel on Cup final day. It was another idiosyncrasy that made the FA Cup final special – the chance to catch a glimpse of the teams in an area that was otherwise *strictly* off limits.

The tunnel was an almost mythical area. The gladiator in all of us dreamed of making that transition from dark into light – from the gloomy tunnel area to the brilliant light of the colosseum. The tunnel was a place of mystery and, sometimes, danger – especially if Roy Keane and Patrick Vieira were knocking about. We devoured stories of tunnel bust-ups, of name-calling, punch-ups and food-fights (although throwing pizza slices at each other was a bit wet when you think about it).

Occasionally, these bundles still occur, though they are rarely captured by the plethora of TV cameras. The most memorable tunnel-brawl in recent years occurred in the Champions League in 2007 in the match between Inter and Valencia. The match will for ever be remembered for the Benny Hill-esque chase around the pitch as the Inter players tried to catch Valencia sub, David Navarro, who – still dressed in his ridiculous grey tracksuit – had run on the pitch and broken the nose of Nicolas Burdisso. The brawl in the tunnel was almost as good: television footage shows an almighty ruckus, with the Inter players trying to storm the Valencia dressing room to get hold of Navarro, who had taken refuge in the showers. This is what tunnels are all about. Tunnels represent the seedier side of our great game. Sadly, they have now been reduced to being somewhere to conduct post-match interviews and keep out of the rain.

The mystique of the tunnel may have been destroyed, but the authorities could, at least, ditch the ridiculous plastic caterpillars. Instead of sportsmen heading back to the sanctuary of the dressing room for a bollocking or a celebratory beer, they look embarrassingly like giant sperm disappearing into an enormous femidom. We can only hope that the retractable tunnel goes the same way as the female condom. Though – however unwieldy – at least the femidom served a purpose.

Turin Shroud

Raised on a diet of the *Daily Mirror*, we can't help loving tabloid journalism. But sometimes the clichés wear us down, particularly when it comes to transfers.

You see, there's only so many times we can imagine Harry Redknapp arranging another 'raid' on his old club or Martin O'Neill 'swooping to sign' some obscure Scandinavian defender. There's only one person in football who should be authorised to swoop for signings, and that's the bonkers Colombian bloke in the bird suit that we used to see suspended from various parts of the stadium during World Cup games. Given a bit of encouragement and a ten per cent cut of the transfer fee, we're pretty sure he would actually bloody *swoop*.

But the worst of these transfer word crimes has to be the 'unveiling' of new signings. How many times have you picked up a paper or turned on the radio to find that some nondescript club will be 'unveiling' some nondescript signing later that afternoon. Are they ever unveiled? No, they bloody well aren't. Are they frogmarched in front of the assembled media with a dust-sheet covering them from head to toe, with the manager pulling on a rope to reveal his latest over-priced acquisition? No, they aren't. Is the unveiling followed by polite but slightly subdued applause? No. But it should be.

We think every new signing *should* be unveiled. Properly. And not just to a couple of world-weary hacks from the local paper. Either do it in the centre circle prior to a game, wheeling the new signing out on one of those low-level trolleys you get at garden centres or, even better, get the local mayor to do it in the town centre at lunchtime. It would give office workers something to gawp at while they stand in the queue at Greggs. For really big signings, there could be marching bands, speeches and maybe an old-fashioned street party. It could be a real shot-in-the-arm for the credit-crunched masses.

All this talk of unveiling has got us thinking: when Ian Rush signed for Juventus in 1987, he could have been draped in the Turin Shroud – that really would've been something special.

So, if we are going to insist on new signings being 'unveiled', then for gawd's sake let's do it properly.

Turnstiles

Turnstiles – the not-so-pearly gateway to your footballing mecca.

There was a time when going through the turnstiles was a matchday rite of passage, up there with standing on a milk-crate or drinking your first cup of Bovril. Now, thanks to the introduction of barcodes and swipe cards, it is a joyless, perfunctory experience. Getting into the match has been reduced to something as banal as getting on the tube or swiping your loyalty card at the supermarket. Not that this surprises us; after all, it is all part of some hidden government agenda to make football as soulless as possible.

We'll be honest: we miss the gruff interaction you used to get with the bloke on the turnstile as you handed over your cash. And we miss the hilarity of some hapless punter trying to get change for a dodgy looking £50 note (and the embarrassed backwards shuffle out of the turnstile that inevitably followed this failed transaction).

With the nation in the grip of recession and unemployment on the rise, what the hell are all these unemployed 'entry facilitation operatives' going to do? Apart from being completely deaf or massively overweight (how did they squeeze into those tiny booths?), there were only two qualifications for being a turnstile operator: possessing absolutely zero social skills; and the ability to indulge in a bit of 'creative book-keeping'. It will never be proven, but we are pretty sure that the blokes on the turnstile – when given the nod from the chairman – were partial to a bit of accounting of the 'one, two, skip a few… ninety-nine, one-hundred' variety.

For all our cynicism, we loved the simple interaction we had with these fellas. It was all part of the football experience. And it added an extra level of excitement to going to the match – you could never be quite sure if these strange, caged psychopaths would give you your change or kill you.

Turnstile operators – we miss you. Though in reality, you've probably just been retrained and re-skilled and now form part of the formidable army of fluorescent-jacketed militia intent on confiscating the lid of your Coke bottle as you enter the stadium (see Bottle Top Old Bill).

TV infidelity – No. 2:
This Is Your Life

Trying to spot footballers on TV shows used to be a real sport. We are not talking about *Match of the Day* or *Sportsnight*. We are talking about TV shows when they weren't actually *playing* football. There were two shows that came up trumps every time, giving footballers a chance to show a different side to their football persona – *This Is Your Life* and *Superstars*.

First up was *This Is Your Life*, which targeted celebrities. This was no modern-day wannabe-celeb-fest, with past-their-sell-by-date stars looking to rekindle their flagging careers. It was a genuine homage to the stars of the day, filmed for the benefit of the public who did not have any access to the lifestyles and friends of the rich and famous. Sportsmen were often the targets of the show and footballers were great as you could guarantee a splattering of teammates, with one or two guaranteed to make a vocal contribution to the proceedings. And like soap-weddings or funerals, you could guarantee a fair smattering of drama. There was the obligatory celebrity colleague who would be filmed somewhere vaguely tropical looking, raising a glass to absent friends – but this was just a ruse, and they'd normally stroll through the double doors right at the end of the show.

For football-mad kids *This Is Your Life* was an opportunity to see their idols out of their normal habitat. A number of footballers received the honour, including George Best, Gordon Banks, Bobby Charlton and Matt Busby.

As a massive Kenny Dalglish fan, Shaun was over the moon when King Kenny finally got his turn. As a final guest, Shaun was hoping for a football superstar or at least an old PE teacher who taught him how to use his big arse. It certainly was a surprise when in strolled, wait for it… Petula Clark! You know, of *Downtown* fame. Apparently, she was a massive fan and family friend. Talk about anti-climax. Based on that, Allan Clarke would have been a result. It was embarrassing for Kenny and for Shaun. How could Shaun face his school friends, and how could Kenny face his teammates? It was a total disaster.

Ironically a footballer was the first to turn down the red book – Danny Blanchflower. We think he must have got wind of his final, surprise, guest.

TV Infidelity No.2: *Superstars*

If one TV programme captured the imagination of sports-mad youngsters everywhere it was *Superstars*. Everyone knew the theme tune.

The premise was this: sign up a few athletes from various sports to compete in a number of events against each other and give points out on a sliding scale. At the end of the series, have a final. Simple. Genius.

This was another show that allowed you to see sport stars in a different arena, and get to know them a bit more. The show, which originally ran from 1973 to 1985, was adapted from American TV (although David Vine claims to have thought up the concept with a group of other broadcasters and sportsmen, but the BBC turned him down, before buying the rights from the US). The show was popular and crucially featured stars at the peak of their sport, who took the competition seriously. The modern reincarnation of the show does not feature current sport stars and doesn't do justice to the original.

Think of *Superstars* and you think of Brian Jacks. His sport was judo, but in *Superstars* he set amazing standards in the gym tests, which involved squat thrusts and his speciality, the dips. He was twice British and twice European winner of the show, and captured the British public's imagination, even having his own computer game.

There were a number of footballers who took part, but none actually won. The closest any came was Colin Bell in 1973 who finished third. A retired Geoff Hurst finished eighth (and last) in 1979, while Mick Channon finished seventh and fifth. Malcolm McDonald, who finished fourth one year, recorded the second fastest sprint in the show's history with a time of 10.9 seconds.

Is it a surprise that a footballer didn't win? Footballers essentially run at different speeds over a long period, but lack upper body strength when compared to other sports. Although competitive, they did not have the all-round fitness to compete with some of the other sportsmen involved.

By far the best piece of football-related *Superstars* action concerned Kevin Keegan, who was competing in a European edition of the show in 1976. Keegan was known as a real competitor and was supremely fit, so it is no surprise that he won his heat. In the cycling event a memorable piece of footage was filmed. Kevin was straining to overhaul his rival, when he crashed at high speed, cutting and grazing his arms and shoulder in a nasty fall. His outfit of a vest and skimpy shorts offered little protection. It is grisly to watch, but ask anyone what they remember about *Superstars* and most will recall this incident. Amazingly he asked to race again and actually finished second in the cycling.

Unfortunately, the show no longer has top stars competing for a number of reasons that we shall not go into. I am sure there are many footballers we would like to see fall off a bike at high speed, or burn their feet while completing squat thrusts, but sadly we are unlikely to have the opportunity. The top football stars may be on our screens more today, but do the programmes allow the public to identify and empathise with them in the same way? The answer is no.

TV rights and wrongs

We can't keep up with who covers what on the telly. We know Sky have got all the decent stuff sewn up, and Setanta used to cover some England games, but not all of them (and never quite enough to tempt us into a subscription, which probably hastened their demise), but when it comes to the FA Cup we're snookered – or, at least, we were…

The FA Cup might be sponsored by E.ON, but what bloody channel is it on? It used to be the jewel in the BBC's live-coverage crown, but not any more. ITV and Setanta scooped the rights to screen the FA Cup (and certain England games) until 2010, paying £425 million for the privilege. That's a lot of wonga, but as Mark Sharman, ITV's Director of News and Sport stated: 'This deal is fantastic news for ITV Sport and our viewers.'

ITV didn't have to wait long for the fans to give *their* verdict. In November 2008, just a few months into the new deal, non-League Histon sent the mighty Leeds United crashing out of the competition with a 1-0 win in the second round – and in true romantic style, the winning goal was scored by a postman. But that wasn't the main event: about 15 minutes in – as clear as day – the crowd can be heard singing the ditty: 'ITV is f*****g sh*t, ITV is f*****g sh*t.' It was audible for a good few seconds before someone pulled the plug (it's still on YouTube if you fancy a laugh). The fans had spoken, a handful of them at least. And it was a critique more damning than anything ever espoused by George Melly, or his profane cousin Roger.

ITV were forced to apologise, although it did seem that much of the 'blame' lay with the Leeds fans, who appeared to have 'alf-inched a pitchside microphone.

The trouble didn't end there. ITV were again forced to apologise, when cameras, placed in the dressing room to film the reaction of Histon's players to the third round draw, managed to beam a picture of a naked non-leaguer (there's a charity calendar in there somewhere, folks) to a bemused nation.

As it turned out, these hi-jinks were just a prelude to the great Tic Tac debacle later in the season (see Commercial suicide), but as we sat in front of the telly on a wet November afternoon, we were under the impression that the FA Cup on ITV was going to be an awful lot of fun. And, at the very least, we can now remember exactly what channel it's on.

U is for Undisclosed

Are undisclosed transfer fees the single most pointless and annoying aspect of the modern game? Over the last few years, the undisclosed fee has become almost as fashionable as the ridiculous tattoos worn by football's elite players.

Who's kidding who? And why don't they want us to know? These are the questions that spring to mind every time a transfer fee is left to the imagination. Is it so the fee won't come back to haunt both the club and the player after the move ends in abject failure and a loan spell at Wycombe Wanderers? Or is it an almighty tax dodge? On second thoughts, don't answer that – we think we've worked it out.

All an undisclosed fee really does is annoy supporters – fans desperate to put a price on their new star striker – especially if the two clubs involved are touting wildly different figures in the national press.

Trouble is, the craze has reached endemic proportions. Of the thirty-two transfers that took place on the last day of the January 2009 transfer window nineteen were 'undisclosed', eleven were free transfers and just two – Robbie Keane's move back to Spurs for £12m and Jim McNulty (Stockport to Brighton) for £150,000 – had the balls to go public.

So come on, let's quit the international money-laundering or whatever it is you are up to and go back to good, old-fashioned transfer fees – fees agreed and published by both clubs involved.

Volker Ippig

As kids we'd often wake in the middle of the night – drenched in sweat – having dreamed we'd been bitten by a venomous snake. The dream was always the same: bitten on the forearm, fang marks as clear as day, we'd be rushing around the jungle screaming for an antidote. Then we'd wake up, usually with pins and needles in the self-same arm. It was scary.

These days, the dreams are similar, except now we wake up dreaming we've been bitten by Ashley Cole.* The sinister, recurring nature of this nightmare has seen us spend countless hours searching the internet for a powerful antivenom. Perhaps we've spent too long watching *Up Close and Dangerous* on Animal Planet, but we live in hope that a crack team of scientists or even Mother Nature herself has developed a cure.

With poor old Ashley Cole personifying everything that is wrong with the modern game – and in light of our nocturnal imaginings – we thought it prudent to seek out an antidote: a footballer politically, ethically, diametrically opposed to Our Ash.

We've searched high and low. We've thought about rubbing our imaginary snake bite with the sweat-soaked shirts of celebrated left-wingers like Cristiano Lucarelli or Lilian Thuram (see *Modern Football is Rubbish*). Then we considered conventional left-wingers like Stewart Downing or Stephen Warnock – but that didn't help much. We considered emailing Javier Zanetti of Inter Milan, who donated £3,400 to the Zapitista rebels in Mexico, or even summoning the spirits of the great managerial socialists-in-the-sky, Bill Shankly and Brian Clough, to ask for advice.

We were looking for a footballer who would refuse to be defined by the size of his pay packet; someone who wouldn't dream of getting married in a white suit; and would refuse to have their wedding photos plastered over the pages of *Hello!* on a point of principle. We were looking for a footballer who could neutralise the effects of a particularly nasty snake bite.

We were just about to give up when we stumbled across Volker Ippig. Volker who? You rightly ask. Volker Ippig is a cult figure at a cult club – and that club is FC St Pauli of Hamburg, a club renowned for it's left-leaning, alternative fanbase, a club with a punk-rock attitude, where football and politics are frequent bedfellows. FC St Pauli stands against all that is wrong with modern football (and modern society) so to be considered a cult (or 'Kult') at St Pauli, you have to have walked the walk – and Volker Ippig certainly has.

After graduating from the FC St Pauli Amateur side (second XI), Volker Ippig decided to take a six-month break from football; not the usual career progression for a player handed a professional contract, but then Ippig wasn't a 'usual' sort of player. Ippig spent his six months 'off' working on the construction of a medical centre in Nicaragua.

Volker also endeared himself to the St Pauli faithful by sharing a squat on the famous Hafenstraße (Harbour Street) in St Pauli. The fate of the famous squatted tenements on the Hafenstraße contributed much to the politicisation of the area and the football club, situated just a few streets away. The punks, squatters and anarchists started attending matches at the Millerntor stadium, and their politics stuck. These fans never forgot Volker – the man who lived on the Hafenstraße and stood side by side with punks, squatters and anarchists in protests against the redevelopment of the area; and who rode to training on a push-bike. FC St Pauli and Ippig graduated to the Bundesliga, where his name was chanted passionately by the Millerntor faithful.

Pre-match, Volker would emerge to conduct his solo pitch inspections and exchange clenched-fist salutes with his comrades in the stands. The fans produced T-shirts with the legend 'Volker hear the signals', a cheeky play on words from the chorus of *The Internationale*. To think, they say that the Germans don't have a sense of humour – pah!

Volker was forced to retire from football with a back injury in 1992, and has since coached at various levels. There have also been unconfirmed reports of him working on the docks in Hamburg. Whatever he is up to now, the man from 'Harbour Street' remains a kult legend in northern Germany. We also think that he's the footballer most likely to provide the antivenom to the 'Ashley Cole Snake Bite Nightmare' that haunts us on a nightly basis.

Volker Ippig didn't win the FA Cup (or German equivalent) once, let alone five times; he didn't move from one side of London to the other for a few dollars more; and we're pretty sure he never married an Atomic Kitten… Oh, hang on, don't we mean a Girl Aloud? Yes, we've decided Volker Ippig is the perfect, soothing antidote to a bite from Ashley Cole – a dock leaf to a stinging nettle.

As a result, we ended up paying £3.68 on eBay for an autographed trading card bearing Ippig's photograph. And, every night, we leave it propped up by the side of the bed – just in case our sleep is disturbed and our dreams have us being bitten by a venomous snake.

* We'd like to point out, in no uncertain terms, that we really don't believe Ashley Cole would bite anyone – this whole scenario is just a product of broken sleep and a vivid imagination. Ashley Cole is used for illustrative purposes only. We don't even really think that he is personally responsible for everything that is wrong with the modern game – that would be a bit silly.

Vote-rigging

We are not interested in vote-rigging at the highest echelons of the game – we'll leave that to Andrew Jennings. Our tales of corruption and influence occur at a much more mundane level and usually involve the internet and some football kit designs. It's the perfect crime for 'the noughties', requiring you to do no more than fire off a couple of emails.

Yes, at some point in the last decade, a bright spark in marketing decided to give the power back to the people. He or she thought it would be a great idea to organise a fan vote for next season's kit.

This involved putting three or four kit designs in the matchday programme or on the internet and allowing fans to vote for their favourite.

For football clubs it was a win-win situation: by presenting the fans with a choice it showed that the club actually cared about their opinions; and it helped the club legitimise another kit change, less than nine months after the last one – it's okay if we fleece you for another £40, isn't it? After all, we did let you choose.

This was a great idea in principle. Unfortunately, it had one fundamental flaw – it didn't take into account one of the defining factors of football fandom: rivalry. Bitter, entrenched rivalry between clubs, that doesn't border on hatred – it embraces it.

Add rivalry to democracy and you've got sabotage. Rival fans aren't put off by having to pay 39p a minute to register their phone vote – not if it means their local rivals playing an entire season in lime green and fucshia. Hell, most fans would re-mortgage their house for that sort of opportunity. Internet voting is even worse: as soon as the word leaks out to a football messageboard, rival fans can change the course of history with the click of a mouse. Sure, it's childish, but it is kind of fun too.

So, sod your *Blue Peter* scandal, or the mysterious goings on in Florida 2005. Vote-rigging on an industrial scale is endemic in English football, and chances are you are a part of it – you tinkers.

World turned upside down

'You'll Never Walk Alone' might've been conceived by Rodgers and Hammerstein, popularised by Gerry and the Pacemakers and adopted by The Kop, but in truth, it belongs to all of football. Let's face it, whatever team we follow, we've all stood at some point with scarves aloft at the end of a game and belted out an emotional version of the song.

A good rendition of 'You'll Never Walk Alone' gives you goosebumps and, as an entire end of the ground stands and sings as one, a sense of unity, unlike any other – for a brief moment mankind is an eternal brotherhood, at peace with each other and united through song.

This is all very well when you are at the match and in the moment, but how many times have you been watching 'You'll Never Walk Alone' being sung on the telly only for the occasion to be ruined by numbskull fans holding their scarves aloft – *upside down*?

For us, it ruins the moment – a bit like your missus shouting out the name of a former lover while on the job (although at least some idiot holding their scarf upside down doesn't usually result in a protracted, messy and expensive divorce).

But it could be stopped. Surely, it is not beyond the remit of responsible scarf manufacturers to print a 'This Way Up' label on the reverse of the scarf? It would eliminate the problem overnight and we could enjoy a hearty rendition of 'You'll Never Walk Alone' without the nagging doubt that it was us holding our scarves the wrong way up.

Other books from SportsBooks

William Garbutt – The Father of Italian Football
Paul Edgerton
In Italy managers are called "mister" and the habit goes back to William Garbutt, who, unable to play any more following injury at the age of 29, went from Blackburn Rovers to coach Genoa. He also coached Roma, Napoli, AC Milan and Athletic Bilbao during a career which also saw him help coach the Italian national team. This fascinating story shows, however, that Garbutt was unknown in his own country.
9781899807826
£7.99
Paperback

A Develyshe Pastime
Graham Hughes
The modern game of football is thought to have its origins in 12th century England. Certainly once the Victorians began organising it in the latter half of the 19th century it spread around the world in various forms. American and Canadian football, Rugby League and Union, Aussies Rules and Gaelic football all have their roots in the rough games played between villages in mediaeval England. Graham Hughes traces the paths the various disciplines took and profiles the men who turned them into major sports.
9781899807796
£17.99
Hardback

Chapped Legs and Punctured Balls
Paul Cooper lived for football like most other 1960s

kids and this is his account, both hilarious and nostalgic, of the things that went with the game in those more innocent times – the clothes and shoes kids wore, the balls they played with, from the very rare leather case ball with its occasionally crippling lace to the stone that was used in the playground if nothing else was available.

9781899807871

£5.99

Paperback

Passport to Football

Stuart Fuller, author of four books of travel guides to football and a well-known blogger on football related matters, brings together his experiences on watching football in far-flung places too numerous to mention here, although they do include Moscow, Macedonia, Klagenfurt, Budapest, and Kazakhstan.

Stuart brings an experienced and humorous eye to the business of watching the beautiful game, noting for example that in a game between Istanbul BBS and Rizaspor an offside goal was allowed to stand because the linesman was arguing with the bench of the team against which he had just given a free-kick!

9781899807833

£12.99

Paperback

Tales from the Gwladys Street

Fans have been having a rough time of it in recent years. Clubs have hiked their admission prices while TV demands have resulted in odd kick-off times which often mean difficult journeys. But still they flock to football matches. This book tells the story of one club, Everton, through the mouths of their fans and players. The resulting stories show how

obsessive football fans can be and how they seek humour in every situation. The stories are from Evertonians but the type of experiences recalled are not unique to one club.
9781899807895
£12.99
Paperback

Finn McCool's Football Club

Stephen Rea was a typical ex-pat in the US. The former Belfast journalist needed somewhere to watch and play football (or soccer as they insist on calling it over there). He found Finn McCool's Irish bar where a diverse collection of nationalities made up the regulars and the football team. They even began to get serious, joining a league. But then Hurricane Katrina struck. Rea's book is both a wry look at an obsession with football and an account of what happened to some of those who suffered one of the US's worst disasters, with an official death toll of 1,100. Many of the team and pub regulars were among those affected by the tragedy.
9781899807864
£8.99
Paperback

Memories of George Best

Chris Hilton & Ian Cole
Malcolm Brodie, of the *Belfast Telegraph* who covered George Best throughout his brilliant and ill-starred career, called this "the best Best book ever". The authors talked to many of the Manchester United star's contemporaries to find out the true story of the wayward genius.
9781899807574
Price £14.99
Paperback